P9-CJM-310

CRUISING THE CALIFORNIA DELTA

BY ROBERT E. WALTERS

This is a book about family cruising —a very rewarding recreation. It is with warmth and a deep sense of privilege that I dedicate it to my own family and regular cruising crew, Erma and Dave. They have been aboard through seasons and assignments spanning 35 years—actively a part of my occupation. The requirements of my pen and the lens, not their preferences of destination, have always dictated to our compass and timepiece. They have been ever patient, always helpful with my preoccupation with print and pictures.

And, it should be especially noted, Erma has had an integral share in this particular presentation's development and preparation. Blessings . . .

Bob Walters

Library of Congress Catalog Card Number 72-78928
International Standard Book Number 0-87930-014-0

Copyright © 1972 by Miller Freeman Publications, Inc.

Lithographed in the United States of America by Levison McNally Company, Reno, Nevada
First impression, May, 1972
Second impression, August, 1972

Delta charts & maps

CONTENTS

Appendix

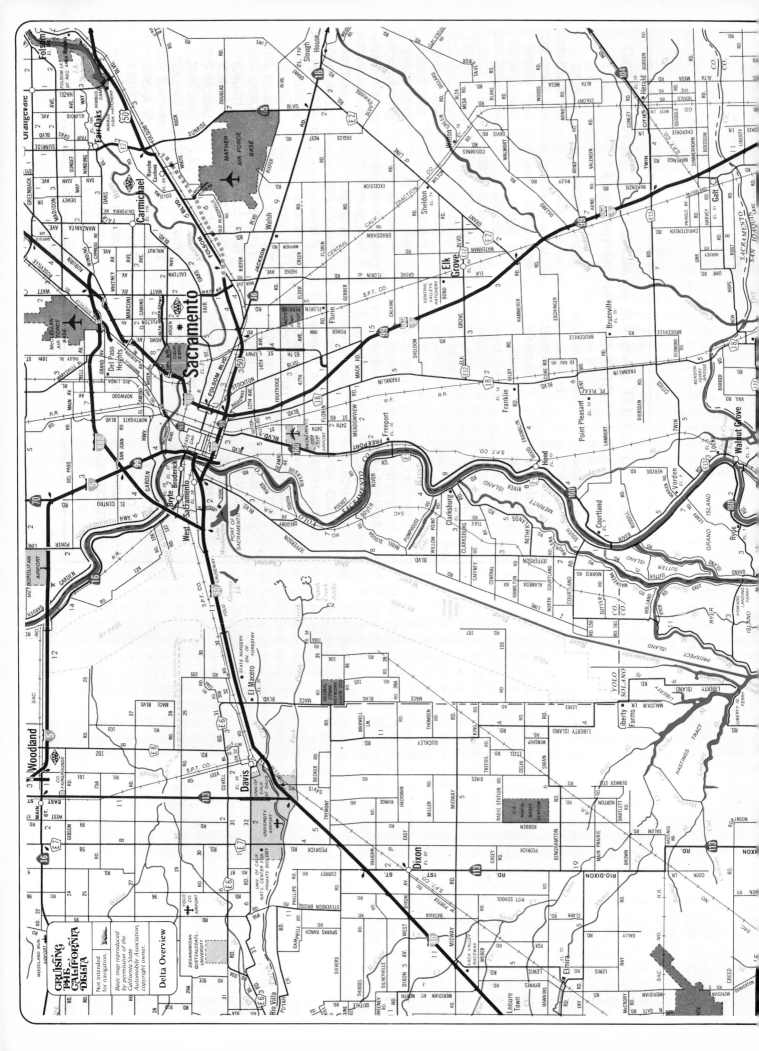

CRUISING
THE
CALIFORNIA
DELTA

Basic map reproduced
by permission of the
California State
Automobile Association,
copyright owner.

Not intended
for navigation.

Delta Overview

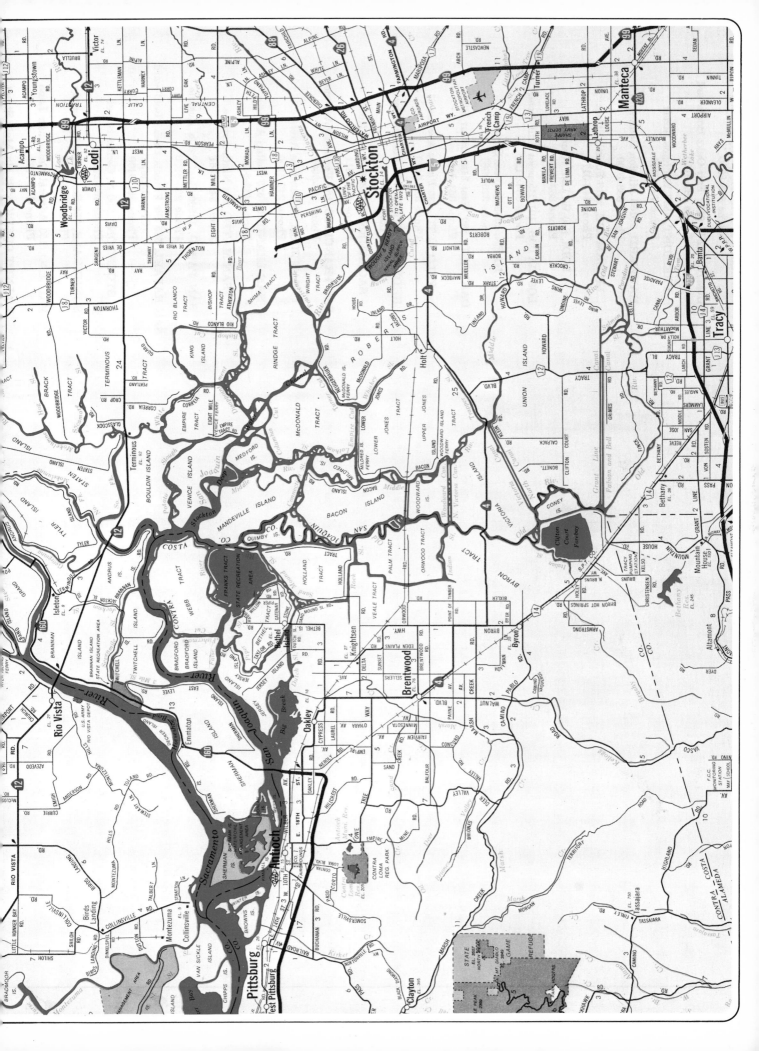

The lofty wheelhouse of the Navajo now overlooks Delta farmland, her hull high and dry inside the levees she helped save.

The rivers of the Delta flow through a fantastic, nature-rich lowland system of water in the great basin of Northern California.

The sources of the Delta rivers are high in the mountains. Down where those mountain-rising rivers are a part of the California spectrum, they wind along at near sea level, through the beds of tules, past the levees and green stands of willows, cottonwoods and sycamore trees.

Intricate green-water patterns bend around grassy berms of marsh mud. Inviting coves, harbors and crescent-shaped anchorages are created by the flows of water against the lowlands, not by relentless seas against rocky headlands and sandy spits.

The levees set the courses. There are several thousand miles of routes between the mudbanks, made stout after a century of battling valley floods. Through these green flat-country corridors pass yachts and pleasure boats by the tens of thousands.

These are the same riverways that once accommodated the riverboats of the old West, the only practical form of water transportation of the time. The West's greatest era of steamboating developed in the California Delta. When this era passed, the armadas of recreational boats took over.

From this new cruising use of the Delta's rivers has come the popular phrase, "a thousand miles of Delta," an informal but realistic appraisal of the distances involved.

Introduction to the Delta

On the Mokelumne, a bridge reflects upon itself in the river waters.

*A street in Locke, originally
the old Delta Chinese settlement,
shows the ravages of time.*

Lowland river country takes a boatman's patient understanding. Sloughs move slowly. The characteristics of the scenery are subtle. The camera, from river level, does not often do justice to the area's beauty. There are no towering peaks. The skipper cannot write breathlessly of standing at the bow, facing ancient battlements along rocky cliffs. There are no vast seas bluer than the skies; no sounds rise aft from hissing wakes.

But the Delta rivers have advantages. They embody boating pleasures not found elsewhere. Pleasure-boat people find a new ease and relaxation in river life and become sensitive to the subtlety of the scenery.

The Delta is distinctively different from any other cruising spot. All of this water is in an intricate, interlocking system within a geographical rectangle that is amazingly compact.

Yet this riverboating differs from the boating connected with the fabled giants, the Mississippi and the Missouri. Our California Delta is far more suited to the growth and present requirements of water recreation.

In our cruising of this area, the skippers and the members of their family crews whom we have met are unanimous in their enthusiasm for their Delta vacations. Samuel T. Clemens, as Mark Twain, wrote in his book, *Life on the Mississippi*, the philosophical comment, "The world and the books are so accustomed to use, and over-use, the word 'new' in connection with our country that there is nothing old about it."

Clemens was chiding the people about their preoccupation with progress at a time when his beloved steamboats were on the wane. He would approve of the Cali-

fornia Delta today. A century later, many of the Delta facilities still carry the marks of age to contrast with the new, modern boats and boating facilities. Neither old nor new dominates on the Delta and the blend is a desirable one. The Sacramento River area is full of the nostalgia that comes from the memories of the days of paddle wheels and settlers. The feeling is rural and there is a surprising remoteness from the metropolitan influences that are actually very close by.

Few frontiers were more colorful than those of the Delta. The waterways were the main trails. They provided the means for the exploration, prospecting and settling of the land. The rivers and sloughs made this countryside's early progress possible. Steamboats replaced the dusty wagons, picking up where the ocean-going ships unloaded their cargoes and passengers.

There are touches of nostalgia around every bend. Sometimes it is a line of old pilings. These once elevated dozens of landings for the steamboats bringing the seeds, machinery and supplies. On the return trips, the boats carried the products to market. In other places, an old boat, or the protruding, mushy ribs of a partly sunken hull will remind the Delta vacationer of the area's colorful past.

Part of the enjoyment of the Delta requires that one get ashore to visit the other side of the levees. The river towns are closely woven into California's history. The two major cities of Sacramento and Stockton are well-known but the smaller towns are worth the visitor's time, too. Antioch, Walnut Grove, Locke, Courtland, Isleton and Rio Vista should all be on the vacationer's time-ashore agenda.

In many of their streets are the aging signs of grander days. Old trading stores, old banks and public buildings still survive. These towns were the middle ground between the commerce of the rivers and the produce from the soil. Unfortunately, most of their great river depots, which once lined the levee banks, are gone.

This is not a pleasure-boating land for the skipper who is in a hurry. The waterways provide opportunity for an enjoyable form of river ratting. The river rat is first a happy man, satisfied with his lot. He spends all his leisure hours along the rivers. It may seem to be a solecism to speak of yachtsmen in that vein. But, invariably, the pleasure-boating skippers who enjoy the rivers are proud of their ability to find the ultimate in shoreside pleasures while bog-bumping up the sloughs every chance they get.

Along with this quest for enjoyable cruising, harbor hopping and shoreside exploration is the great variety of other recreational boating pursuits. The smooth waters and extraordinarily long courses of the Delta have turned this area into one of the greatest water-skiing attractions in California. Fishing is exceptional. The

An anchorage in the Delta is where you find it. Tree trunks are your mooring buoys.

many bait and tackle shops attest to the fisherman's enthusiasm for the area.

Gunkholing and easy cruising can become a special kind of scenic experience. Here and there you will encounter an old bow poking out of tule stalks, splashing in your wake. There are little sheds tumbling from their pilings, just waiting for the appreciative eye of a passing sketchbook artist. On stretch and turn, the tules and willows contrast with the sleek hulls of the pleasure boats drawn up to them.

To revel in the Delta's past is to idle-down the boat and imagine the river life as it used to be.

There are the old tales of the early Chinese field workers who tallied the loading of crates and sacks with the abacus, the venerable Oriental calculating machine. The captains were impatient and the gangplanks would be withdrawn without a final settlement. The air was filled with noise and profanity in two languages. It ranks as the Delta's earliest "communication gap."

"Steamboat round the bend . . ." was a familiar cry along Steamboat Slough, the Sacramento and the San Joaquin. There are stirring stories of great pride for the rival steamboats and many informal river races were staged. Scheduled trips were suddenly sold out as word got around that a race between favorites was shaping up.

These races sometimes ended in tragedy. Boilers and machinery would not take the strain. There were explosions and crashing timbers, fires and many deaths. Newspapers railed against the laxities and underscored this frightful, devil-may-care attitude of the river boatmen. Finally, order came to the water traffic on all of the big Delta rivers.

The recipe for cruising enjoyment in the California Delta is a mix of one part river water and greenery, one part the atmosphere from the old times and one part the multitude of places to roam that are so ideally suited to our modern-day recreational boating.

In 1772, the expedition party led by Fray Juan Crespi and Pedro Fages looked down from Mount Diablo. They saw two great rivers and a vast valley of sloughs, peat and natural vegetation. They were the first white men to record the discovery of the Delta. The Spanish explorers were impressed with the hundreds of water routes, the great stands of tules, the variety of game and waterfowl and the many small but lushly grown alluvial islands. They came first to explore and establish missions. It is ironic that, eighty years later, the rivers they first saw from Diablo would bear great treasures of gold, the kind of wealth that Spain's kings had sought in vain elsewhere throughout the hemisphere.

While many of the Delta's regional names are drawn from the Spaniards and the Indians, many more are from the idiom of the early settlers. They had earthy reasons to come up with names like Hog Slough, Potato Slough, Fisherman's Cut and Deadhorse Island.

Top: The Mokelumne provides a quiet interlude, the temperature 90° but the shade a rich, green cool. Below: Miles of levees, trees, tules, willows and gentle water.

The Indians in these river valleys were peaceful and pursued, in common with most other coastal tribes, lives of hunting, fishing and farming. There were occasional battles with the exploring parties but it was the great epidemic of fever in 1833 that took the heaviest toll, almost obliterating the Delta tribes.

There were over 30,000 Indians living in the valley, nearly half of them close to the rivers. It is estimated that two-thirds of them died in the 1833 epidemic, believed to have been a form of malaria brought in by boat.

It was the Chinese who provided the great labor pool required for the massive human effort that built the first levees. The Chinese also helped work the rich farmland. They were shipped in by the thousands. Many hundreds more moved over from the railroad building gangs. There are no records of the total numbers of this huge, low-wage work force. Along the levees the Chinese wielded the tule cutters in the peat, pushing the cuttings out of the muck on crude wheelbarrows in order to tamp the peat squares into place.

Then the famous Fresno Scraper was developed. This was a huge, horsedrawn scraping shovel with big handles and a dumping catch. The Fresno Scraper worked on both the levees and the early western roads.

Very few of the old Chinese settlers are left in the Delta. Of their many main settlements, only the old buildings at Locke and Walnut Grove survive.

Tules, berms and fogs are among the most common terms of the Delta region. "Tule" does not rhyme with "rule," it is pronounced "tooly." The name was originally given a specie of bullrushes growing where the soil had been overflowed in the southwestern United States and adjacent Mexico. Tules are perennials. Webster now recognizes the tule as native to Northern California.

The Spanish explorers noted these ten-foot stalks growing profusely in Delta country. They were so impressed with these great seas of tules they called the region "Tulares." Tulare, California, is now a prominent San Joaquin valley town, perpetuating the Spanish name.

The chart makers came along and called the midstream outcroppings tule islands. There are stories that the Indians bundled the tule stalks into rafts to cross the sloughs, the same method used by the Egyptians with the Nile's bullrushes.

The clinging tule fogs each winter are infamous. These fogs are a special brand of thick stuff that hangs low to the ground for days when the dew point is reached and the atmosphere vaporizes from the warmth of the land. A Northern Californian calls every thick, ground-hugging fog a tule fog and will match the Delta region's fogs against London's finest.

Berm is another prominent word in the Delta. It is

Heading out from a little gunkhole in the lee of one of Delta country's many old bridges.

the name given the shelf, or ledge, of the levee below the watermark. Berm is also used for any narrow, grassy ridge that creates a channel variance.

This particular boating family's long friendship with the Delta began in 1962. Prior to that summer's trip, we had spent years cruising the saltchucks of Puget Sound, the San Juan Archipelago and the gorgeous island and mountain country of western British Columbia.

Ours was the *Davy W.*, a fast, mobile little cruiser carrying 21,000 nautical miles in her logbooks from these writing and photographing expeditions of cruising pleasure in the grandeur of the Pacific Northwest.

In moving to our Southern California headquarters, we set our cruising sights on the Delta. Curiosity was the primary motivation. We trailered the boat by highway, then hung *Davy W.* from a crane boom at Bethel Island and dipped her into the waters where three sloughs join. There have been many boating visits to the Delta since, topped by three separate cruises in 1971, updating material and acquaintanceships for the purpose of this book.

Our crew has an honest fondness for the Delta, its people and the visiting boating men it attracts. We who had developed strong ties and a boating love for the scenic Pacific Northwest now boast an equal attachment to the southern coastlines.

On the flood of the tide, a bonsai arrangement.

As a boating family cruising along these intriguing rivers and sloughs, we have been given that warm sense of belonging. Our status is still that of visitors but, as our skipper, I have become an enthusiastic, self-appointed Delta ambassador without portfolio.

The ensuing chapters are predicated on the belief that the waterways of the California Delta are truly magnificent in their own style and character.

Rivers are always slow to change. They have a natural resistance to it. This is their special beauty, their worth. The Delta's waterways have acted in the same way. They have absorbed the coming of the great fleets of pleasure boats and the crews that man them with equanimity. It has made little difference. They flow quietly along, letting the pleasure-bound boat-borne guests discover the richness and variety of the area for themselves.

This chance to be the discoverer is the charming characteristic of Delta boating. Crowding presents some drawbacks but there are still more places to go than there are small pleasure boats to fill them. Treated properly, it will be that way in the Delta for a long, long time. Having people around can be fun, too. Out there among the tules they are a friendly lot. So, let's weigh the anchor and glide out into the slough and dike country of Northern California—the Delta.

The Rio de Sacramentos has been called the "Nile of the West" and the "River of Gold." Without it the development of California would have been slowed.

Also without it, California's special recreational blessing, the Delta, would not be the same. The river's vast supply of waters and its channels leading to many other courses give us the room to enjoy this natural, interlocking system, which otherwise would be truncated by huge chunks of land.

The river has a rugged, colorful past. It was once known as the Rio de San Francisco. Few among the cruising clans are aware that Gabriel Moraga, the Spaniard and early explorer by whose name we now call the hills adjacent to the lower section of the river, first named this river "San Francisco."

Moraga also originally named the Feather River, El Rios de Los Sacramentos, a confusion of singular and plural. Whether he applied this name to the complex of streams, or whether mistakes were made in recording the phrase, or both, we do not know. The Feather is a tributary to the main river and is significant in the massive California Water Plan. Another explorer came along after Moraga and named the Feather River "Las Plumas," The Feathers, and this took hold. The "Sacramentos," or river of the Sacraments, became the name of the big river that forms the western boundary of the Delta region's watery wonderland.

Water statistics show that one-third of all of the run-off of California streams reaches the ocean through the channels of the 400-mile Sacramento that begins as a little lake high on Mount Eddy. This is a water drop from 14,000 feet to sea level.

The Sacramento

Nile of the West

The Sacramento Yacht Club facility, in the state capital, is on a barge adjacent to its floats.

2

Once gold was discovered near the Sacramento River there was a great and immediate need for freight and passenger service from the San Francisco Bay Area to New Helvetia, the name of the site that is now the capital of the state of California. Originally, because the river was still unspoiled and very deep, every kind of craft was tried in service. Pilots warped sailing vessels upstream with only pencil sketches to serve as charts.

Soon the gold fields had drawn 28 steamers and an assortment of barks and brigantines of more than 60 in number. The year 1850 was a busy one along the Sacramento River.

Colorful as the gold era was, and for all it did in encouraging the settling of California, it also defeated the Sacramento as a river of suitable depths for shipping. Hydraulic mining systems took over and were successful in getting out the gold. Unfortunately this method of mining also sluiced down uncountable tons of mud, silt and debris. The Sacramento filled in part. So did other rivers and sloughs. The great flood of 1862 was devastating and a contributing factor in spreading the silt far and wide. Hydraulic mining was finally banned but not until 1884. The Sacramento remained a river for shallow-draft steamers for a long time.

Later, modern engineering and the big dredges opened the river to deep-sea freighters and cargo barges. Sacramento became a modern seaport.

These commercial ships no longer use the old-river stretches from Rio Vista to Sacramento. Instead they use the big, deepwater channel built expressly for commercial traffic. The gregarious, modern pleasure boats have the old-river section all to themselves.

Whatever the gold mining methods did to harm the rivers of the Delta, they did bring on the era of the steamboat. There was a rush to get the gold from the miners' pokes. Boat passenger business was declining in the northeastern coastal ports of the country so a stampede of sidewheelers headed west. The large ones made dangerous, rough voyages around the Horn. The smaller ones were dismantled and shipped around in the holds of sailing vessels. Reassembly took place in crude Bay Area yards. For those who remember the knock-down pleasure-boat packages for economy buyers, here is the reminder that the idea was working a century earlier.

Today's skipper is fascinated by the historic operations of the old steam-engine riverboats—sidewheel, sternwheel and propeller. Old pictures of the glory days of these river ships are still to be found on occasional

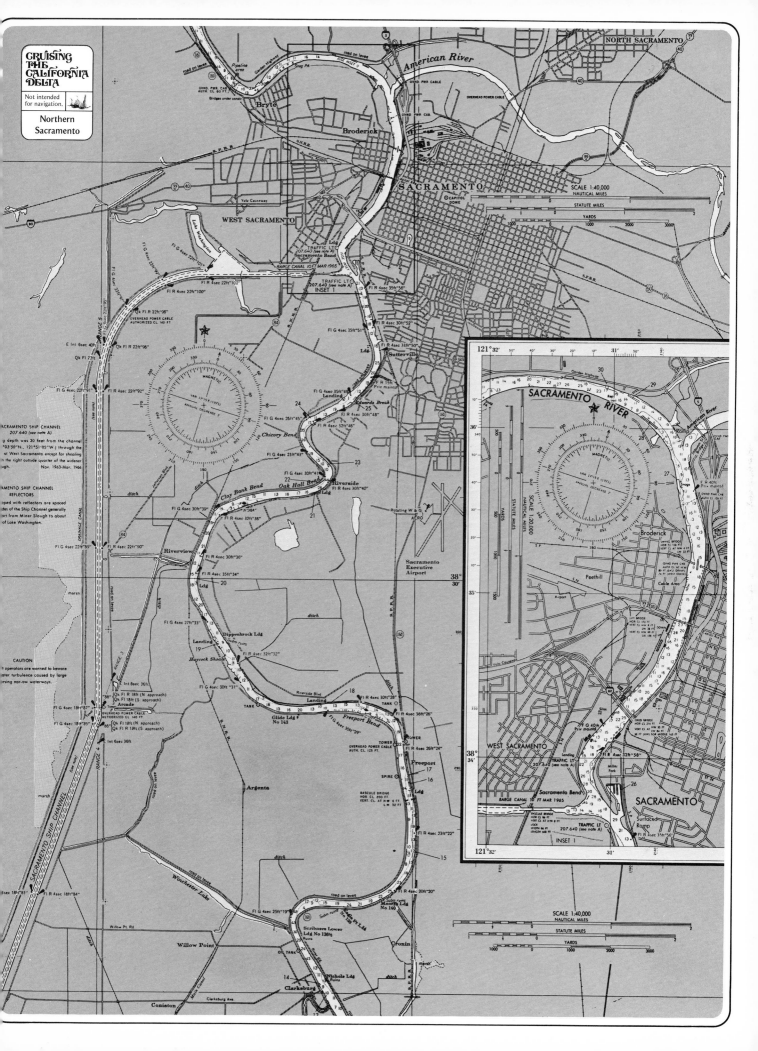

display in Delta marinas, restaurants and taverns. Those were the days of riverboat races, anecdotes of landing activities and, sometimes, a bow aimed full-bore at the side of a competing paddlewheeler.

There were many great names among these early carriers. There were the famous *Senator*, built in New York; the fleet *Antelope,* which carried to the coast the first packet of Pony Express mail to reach Sacramento; the *New World,* which steamed out of New York under debt liens and the noses of the officers enforcing the orders. The *New World* set the speed record for the San Francisco-Sacramento run, broken later by the *Chrysopolis.* Other names famous for their Sacramento-San Francisco runs were the *Nevada, Capital City, Washoe, Yosemite,* the *San Rafael, Jenny Lind, John A. Sutter, Governor Dana, Navajo, C. M. Weber, Camanche, Apache* — the list is long.

The vacationing boatman setting forth on his Sacramento cruise follows in the wake of the river's exciting past.

Plans for a Sacramento River cruise depend upon one's recreational objectives. There are many alternatives beginning with where you decide to start your explorations. There are many starting points between the San Francisco Bay Area shorelines to Sacramento, with many ports and marinas in between.

My own approach is usually from a tule niche or marina harbor on the interior flank of the river. For several seasons, because we live so far away, we kept a comparatively large boat in dry storage at a half-way point. From there, we could fan out conveniently in many directions.

Through our Delta cruises we have come to think of the Sacramento as divided into three distinct sections for cruising. In making this arbitrary division, we are influenced by changes in size, direction, scenery and climate. Each of our three sections gives the skipper a different kind of river for his pleasure-boating experience.

The total course is approximately 75 miles long, generally from Antioch, Pittsburg and Suisun Bay up to the city of Sacramento. We rarely start at either end to cruise the length in a single run. Instead, we enter the river from other sloughs. Our two favorite points for commencing our Sacramento cruises are the Rio Vista area and the Walnut Grove region. Each of these has easy connections with a variety of other cruising patterns.

Our section of the Sacramento starts at the river's mouth and goes up 12 miles to a point of abrupt change in direction a short distance above Rio Vista. Call this section the "broad river" because it is around 1,000 yards wide and none of the rest of the course approaches this width.

The course then makes a sharp 90° turn, but there is a peculiar short stub that the chart makers have left without a designation. Popular Steamboat Slough takes off from the stub. At its termination the water diffuses into a tree-limb pattern of sloughs—Miner, Cache, Prospect—and the major entry into the Sacramento deep-water channel. Stiff cross winds are characteristic of the lower Sacramento. In summer, the same stiff breezes that keep the heat from being unbearable, also rough up the water. Early river explorers made a point of describing the strong winds that blew steadily across the great seas of tules. Large boats get little more than an occasional whip off the spray rail but smaller boats will often be slowed down with some bumping and discomfort.

We approached our own first cruise of the lower section of the Sacramento by coming down the river past Isleton and Ida Island that shelters Vieira's fine marina. We had stayed that night in a protective little notch of a berm on an "inside" slough. We were with friends aboard two other boats. Rio Vista and the lower river were suggested for the next day. As we reached the "broad river" we encountered the long push out to the ship channel markers, only partly avoiding the temptation of shorting it across the covered big spit. We corrected in time but learned from this experience that one must adhere strictly to the main course.

Now we were facing the Rio Vista highway bridge, the biggest, blackest structure on the Delta. Its dull, dark paint makes it look ominous. Its two giant towers for raising the bridge center can be seen for miles.

We were soon abreast of Rio Vista, cruising back and forth along its historic waterfront. Here one day in 1865, just after dark, the famous 283-foot pride of passenger service, the *Yosemite,* was leaving Rio Vista's docks. Many questions were asked later about her steam pressure and safety valve setting. She was just underway when the boiler let go. There was a horrible crush of wood, machinery and humanity. She was carrying a ton of gold but it was salvaged. Five were killed and a number of passengers injured. The survivors were taken into Sacramento by her companion ship on the run, the *Chrysopolis.*

A year before, a few miles above Rio Vista, the *Washoe* had blown up. Soft iron didn't make stout boilers and passengers ran a calculated risk.

We cruised into Rio Vista's Delta Marina to tie up among sleek pleasure boats at bright, clean floats. Owner Jack Baumann has an outstanding marina here, incorporating the well-rated restaurant, The Point, placed where diners overlook the neat little hook into the harbor. It has been our pleasure to be served what we rate as some of the best broiled fresh salmon in Northern California at The Point.

On that first day, Jack arranged for a ride for eight of us into the downtown section of Rio Vista, the largest of the river towns in the middle area of the Sacramento.

*In the river town of Isleton,
the old hall houses a local store.*

*Small boat groups
especially will enjoy the many
pleasant river beaches.*

*In Courtland,
one of the few remaining riverside
warehouses on the Sacramento.*

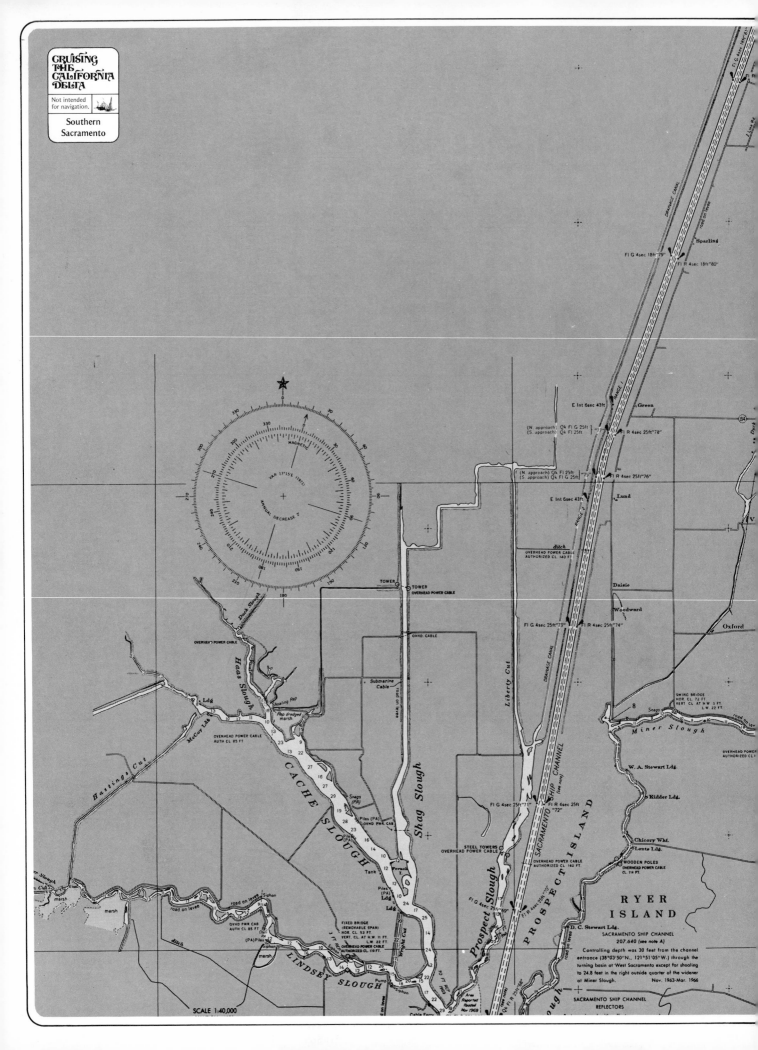

Sparling

FI G 4sec 18ft "79"

FI R 4sec 18ft "80"

E Int 6sec 43ft   Green

(N. approach) Qk FI G 25ft
(S. approach) Qk FI G 25ft   FI R 4sec 25ft "78"

(N. approach) Qk FI G 25ft
(S. approach) Qk FI G 25ft   FI R 4sec 25ft "76"

E Int 6sec 43ft   Lund

OVERHEAD POWER CABLE
AUTHORIZED CL 140 FT

ditch

Daisie

Woodward

FI G 4sec 25ft "73"   FI R 4sec 25ft "74"

Oxford

TOWER   TOWER
OVERHEAD POWER CABLE

OVHD. CABLE

Duck Slough

OVERHEAD POWER CABLE

Haas Slough

Submarine
Cable

Liberty Cut

SWING BRIDGE
HOR. CL 72 FT
VERT. CL AT H.W. 1 FT
LW. 22 FT

Miner Slough

OVERHEAD POWER
AUTHORIZED CL 1

Ldg

Shoaling Rep

Rep dredged
marsh

McCoy Ldg

OVERHEAD POWER CABLE
AUTH CL 85 FT

Hastings Cut

W. A. Stewart Ldg.

Shag Slough

CACHE SLOUGH

Snags (PA)

Piles (PA)
OVHD PWR. CAB.

Kidder Ldg.

SACRAMENTO SHIP CHANNEL

Chicory Whf.

Tank

STEEL TOWERS
OVERHEAD POWER CABLE

Lents Ldg.

OVERHEAD POWER CABLE
AUTHORIZED CL 140 FT

WOODEN POLES
OVERHEAD POWER CABLE
CL 114 FT

PROSPECT ISLAND

Prospect I.

Piles
(PA) Ldg

Prospect Slough

RYER
ISLAND

D. C. Stewart Ldg.

SACRAMENTO SHIP CHANNEL
207.640 (see note A)

Controlling depth was 30 feet from the channel
entrance (38°03'50"N., 121°51'05"W.) through the
turning basin at West Sacramento except for shoaling
to 24.8 feet in the right outside quarter of the widener
at Miner Slough.   Nov. 1963-Mar. 1966

SACRAMENTO SHIP CHANNEL
REFLECTORS

FI G 4sec 25ft "71"   FI R 4sec 25ft "72"

FI G 4sec 25ft "69"

FIXED BRIDGE
(REMOVABLE SPAN)
HOR. CL 53 FT
VERT. CL AT H.W. 11 FT
LW. 22 FT
AUTHORIZED CL 118 FT

OVHD PWR CAB
AUTH CL 85 FT

(PA)Piles

Siphon

road on levee

Siphon

ditch

marsh

LINDSEY SLOUGH

Pump

Cable Ferry

Free
Reported
flooded
Nov 1969

Qk FI R 25ft "70"

Rio Vista's old-time river traffic is gone but it has stores and a number of services. The town could use a protected small-boat landing of size at the foot of its sloping streets for pleasure boaters who now comprise Rio Vista's river-borne commerce.

We were introduced to Foster's Big Horn, an old-time restaurant and bar with immense wall displays of big game mounts. These magnificent displays should be on everyone's things-ashore list. We hope the full display, from the great tusked elephant heads to the mounts of the sleek gazelles, will someday be a part of a Delta museum.

After our day in town, our flotilla cruised on to Antioch for the night and a tour of the marinas clustered on the San Joaquin side of this big junction of the two key Delta rivers. Many large yachts from the Bay Area side are moored there permanently. There is a complete choice of fuel stations, boatyards, repair and sales centers. The Riverview Restaurant, overlooking the complex of rivers, sloughs and islands, is immensely popular in all seasons with both boaters and landlubbers.

Scenically this lower stretch is primarily open river, a place for main-channel movement to somewhere else. There is a little hook of a slough called Three Mile, which is about as long as it is. Three Mile takes off about five miles below what old-timers called "Rio Visty." It is the shortest, most effective route over to the San Joaquin and/or down into the Bethel Island region.

What we call the second division of the Sacramento is easier to explain on the premise of traveling upstream, though the line of demarcation would be the same from either direction.

The Sacramento, at a point just above the Rio Vista Bridge, takes a 90° turn as one makes a heading for Walnut Grove, about 15 miles away. The wide section of river has gained from the water coming down Steamboat Slough, added to its own flow, but once the turn is made you have an entirely different river, narrowed to a third of the width of its lower section. The high levees on each side close in on your boat. The surrounding shore scenery is different. There are many well-aged trees and high, natural-growth shrubbery giving protection from prevailing winds. On many sweeping curves the boatman has a feeling of canyon privacy. Much of the course closely resembles Georgiana Slough scenery. The charts show that the river parallels the slough for several miles.

Georgiana is hidden from sight but actually is only about a thousand yards to the east.

One first sights Ida Island, a big chunk of land with a small slough behind it.

The first big curve carries us past the interesting river town of Isleton, another leftover from steamboat days. Many people keep boats on the Mokelumne shop at Isleton but make the trip by auto. Isleton could use public visitors' floats for the pleasure-boating families who want to stop and shop and do not wish to resort to autos. There could be engineering and usage restrictions on this waterfront due to the lack of an inner harbor, but this could be overcome. Other river cities in the Delta face this same problem. Two such are neighboring Locke and Walnut Grove. Some of the citizens of the Delta river towns are rising to the pleas of yachtsmen.

Altogether the total stretch of these fifteen or so miles, from Rio Vista bridge to Walnut Grove, is a good cruise, rich in olive and apple leaf greens, good for fishing, popular for its lengthy water-skiing runs. The shoreside remnants of the steamboat-landing days provide interesting sightseeing and a rub-rail touch with history.

The boatman will encounter another bridge above Isleton, curtailing boating with its limited high-water clearance. This one isn't too bothersome. But pleasure-boat skippers who know the Delta agree that a good project for all of the state's yachtsmen would be the urging of a program to free the Delta waterways with higher spans and better-attended lifts. The Delta is the biggest, single boating attraction in California inside the saltwater line and it is growing. Its pleasure-boating commerce deserves attention to its needs.

Moving way up, Ryde is on our port, an anachronism. Here begins the sharp swing for the entrance to Georgiana Slough, Walnut Grove's landing and another bascule bridge.

Standing on the Sacramento levee at Walnut Grove, our third section of the river comes into view—the 40 miles to the city of Sacramento which lies ahead. In these forty miles one sees just about everything that can move on the water including sailboats clawing upstream. Expert water skiers gather here for the exceptional long runs on the flat, unimpeded courses.

We chose late September for our cruise to the state's capital, our first in the post-vacation season after vacations deplete the fleets.

Camera bugs aboard will collect their own shots for a Sacramento River page in a Delta album. It might look like this with (upper left) Pipe Dream II—something new on the old river. Top right: Comfortable old homes like this one line the banks. Below, right: Sailboats use motors to reach upstream and trailerboaters make use of one of the many good launching ramps. Bottom, left: In Courtland, a landmark example of old river town architecture and just above it a fast cruise past a rip-rapped levee.

23

*An Islander 24 warps its
slow way up the Sacramento toward Courtland
against a warm late July sun.*

We entered the Sacramento from Georgiana Slough after a stop in the shade near the Isleton bridge for lunch aboard. To detail each bend in the river enroute on the 40-mile course to Sacramento would be cumbersome and unnecessary but some general comments about the route will be helpful. The scenery opens up and temperatures are generally higher than in the lower-river area. There is a nice mixture of the old facilities with the more recent modern developments. We suggest that the vacationing boatman steer a crooked course to take in the interesting things on each side of the river.

There are a number of distinctive river marinas that vary in size and kind. Many include restaurant and snack bar services. Friend and crew member Jess Crowe was along on this trip, out of Spindrift Yacht Club, and he received the yeoman's duty of counting the marinas, coming up with eighteen total. Of these, about eight are major in size and variety of services offered. Among them, at Freeport Bend, the large size and attractive appearance of the popular Freeport Marina stands out.

Go ashore to visit the interesting and historic old river towns of Courtland, Hood, Freeport and Clarksburg. I particularly recommend Courtland, the first of these river towns, just above Walnut Grove. Behind those high levees are streets and old buildings straight out of a rural, 1915 movie set. Along the way, there is also some fascinating architecture in the grand farm estate manner. From your boat these spots can be located by the fine stand of old trees, plantation style, reaching above the river banks.

A reminder of the old days of navigating the Sacramento on the big riverboats is preserved on the newest of the nautical charts, 5528-SC. Each bend is listed by name. A knowledge of this detail was very important to the big riverboat captain who had to be sure precisely where he stood and where to stand off, day and night. The names are regional and colorful: Freeport Bend, Garcia Bend, Clay Bank Bend, Oak Hall and others.

Most of the old landings are gone, but the chart lists every one of them either by name or number. There are approximately 140 separate identification numbers indicating the number of farms that once depended on the call of the freight and passenger steamers. Many are noted on the chart with the legend, "abandoned."

Nearing Sacramento, we took time to enjoy the lovely scenes of the great sweep from Sacramento Bend, past the city and capitol, and in front of the American River. These sections are like a vast city park built around a river. We moved along to what is perhaps the loveliest area of all, around to Bryte, a place where we drifted for

an hour with the current, expecting to hear band concerts from the groves of trees.

This section of one's cruise begins with a glide along Miller Park and a short, surrounding area that is outstanding for its trees and landscaping. Always interesting to boating people is a little hook and entry into the Miller Park Marina. We gassed up here. It is a fine marina in a beautiful setting.

Moving toward downtown Sacramento, the scene changed more to bridges and commercial waterfront stands. The area is cleaner than many such waterfront districts. The Sacramento Yacht Club is an interesting riverfront establishment and worth a visit.

The American River can be used by pleasure boats for only a short distance, but its wide mouth creates a "bay" in the Sacramento. A friend who keeps his boat in the city once said, "There is more beautiful, exciting boating activity in that small circle on weekends than can be imagined."

It was along the American, near its south fork, that James Marshall, an employee of Sutter, spotted gold in 1848 and turned loose the great emigration from the east—men and the steamboats to serve them.

Group cruising and crowded marinas are a way of life on Delta rivers. Top: A marina scene not far from the capitol's dome. Bottom: Visiting boats, Grand Banks cruisers crowd the Delta Marina at Rio Vista.

Now, for all those who love the river history and its stories, either because of their boats or as landlubbers who are California history buffs, a great project is under way. A group of Sacramento citizens, Riverboat's Comin', Inc!, has moored the historic *Delta King* in a permanent berth near Capitol Avenue, not far from the state's headquarters. This group is involved in a preservation and restoration movement to save the fading relic, creating a tourist attraction and museum. Tours of the *Delta King* are available, now offered on Sundays. This civic-minded group is headed up by Captain Ed Morgain, the *Delta King*'s last skipper. His address is 6011 Fairway, Sacramento (916-456-2681). Our chapter on the old riverboats later on in this book carries more details of the *King.* For now, this is a good place to end our cruise of the Sacramento—with a tour of the *Delta King.*

The old and new worlds share the river. Top: Activity on the stretch above Walnut Grove. Bottom: The grand old Sternwheeler, Delta King, *is a floating waterfront museum in Sacramento.*

Pices *follows another boat up a narrow channel near the Snodgrass Slough entry to The Meadows.*

3 Snodgrass

Queen of the Sloughs

Snodgrass Slough could call herself the Queen of all the Delta sloughs.

Although her usable course is only eight miles long, she has a glorious variety of surroundings, some deep wooded, others open. She attracts many boats through short, easily accessible connections with the Sacramento River and its unlimited cruising potentials, and with the several branches of the Mokelumne River, which lead to the Delta's heartland. This tight, inland enclosure, not unlike a lake in parts, is within easy reach of the bays and the open sea beyond.

On some days of the season, Snodgrass is able to harbor everything in the fleet that works toward her. In addition to the huge number of boats anchoring there overnight at the height of the season, many more houseboats, cruisers and recreational craft are active during the sunny hours.

This slough divides into five prominent regions. At the beginning there is a tree-edged reach of river proportions. This has the appearance of an extension of the Mokelumne River which turns off near the Giusti Landing juncture.

Next the Snodgrass meets the Cross Delta Channel, forming an open area that is popular with water skiers. The channel controls the waters flowing back and forth from the Sacramento River and provides low-bridge boats with a time-saving route between the Sacramento and the slough.

Up the slough from this open panorama of water and farmland, the scene changes completely. The courses become narrow and winding as the water is divided by long, narrow tule islands. These islands and the marshy shorelines, where there is no diking, are covered with foliage that is nearly tropical in density. Several courses are available on both the port and starboard and, with care, skippers can find deep enough water for many boats to cross laterally between these narrow reaches. This stretch has all the beauty of muddy green waters and overhanging trees that make the Mexican jungle cruises out of Mazatlan so intriguing.

Skippers who want to cut a fast swath, and lay the water back in a flat, sparkling wake, can take the starboard course and ride the base of the levee. This breaks from its wide and scenic arc into a narrow convergence of muddy water and swishing leaves and a direct ride into The Meadows.

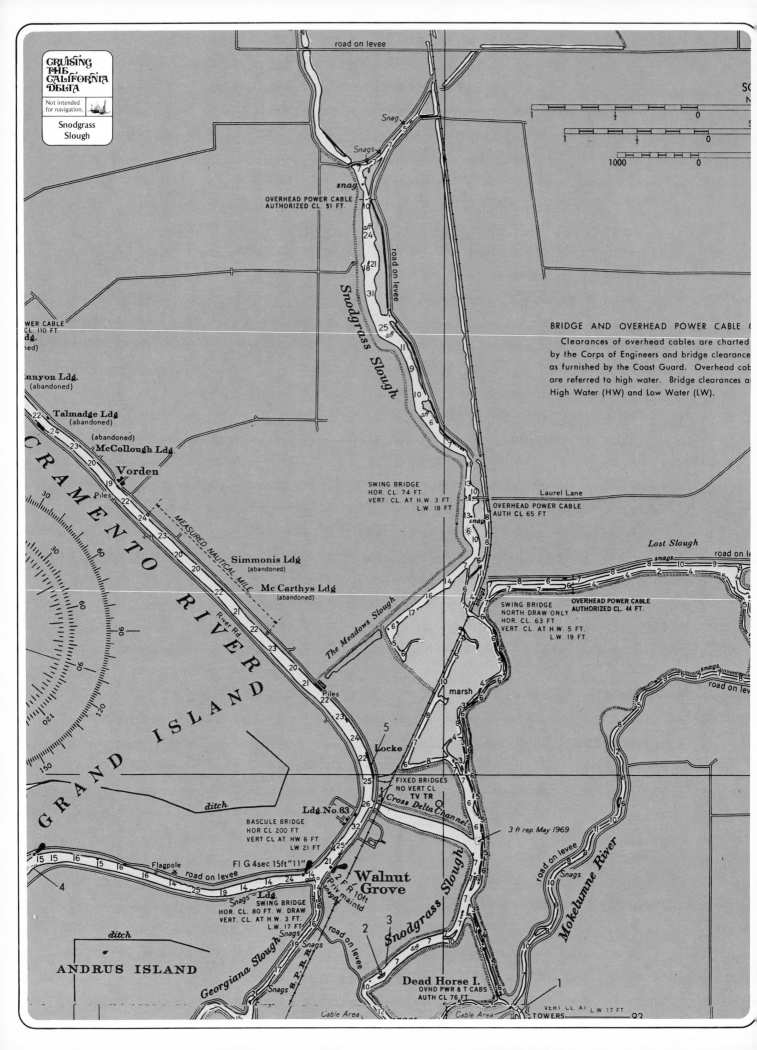

CRUISING THE CALIFORNIA DELTA

Not intended for navigation.

Snodgrass Slough

road on levee

Snag

Snags

snag

OVERHEAD POWER CABLE
AUTHORIZED CL. 51 FT.

Snodgrass Slough

road on levee

BRIDGE AND OVERHEAD POWER CABLE

Clearances of overhead cables are charted
by the Corps of Engineers and bridge clearance
as furnished by the Coast Guard. Overhead cab
are referred to high water. Bridge clearances a
High Water (HW) and Low Water (LW).

WER CABLE
CL. 110 FT.
dg.

anyon Ldg.
(abandoned)

Talmadge Ldg
(abandoned)

(abandoned)
McCollough Ldg.

Vorden

Piles

MEASURED NAUTICAL MILE

River Rd

SACRAMENTO RIVER

GRAND ISLAND

Simmonis Ldg
(abandoned)

Mc Carthys Ldg
(abandoned)

The Meadows Slough

Piles

Locke

SWING BRIDGE
HOR. CL. 74 FT.
VERT. CL. AT H.W. 3 FT.
L.W. 18 FT.

Laurel Lane

OVERHEAD POWER CABLE
AUTH CL 65 FT

Lost Slough

road on le

snags

SWING BRIDGE
NORTH DRAW ONLY
HOR. CL. 63 FT.
VERT. CL. AT H.W. 5 FT.
L.W. 19 FT.

OVERHEAD POWER CABLE
AUTHORIZED CL. 44 FT.

snags

road on lev

marsh

snag

ditch

FIXED BRIDGES
NO VERT CL
TV TR

Cross Delta Channel

3 ft rep May 1969

Ldg. No. 63

BASCULE BRIDGE
HOR CL 200 FT
VERT CL AT HW 6 FT
LW 21 FT

Fl G 4sec 15ft "11"

Flagpole

road on levee

Snags Ldg.
SWING BRIDGE
HOR. CL. 80 FT. W. DRAW
VERT. CL. AT H.W. 3 FT.
L.W. 17 FT.

2 F R 10ft
Priv maintd

snags

Walnut
Grove

Snodgrass Slough

road on levee

Snags

Mokelumne River

ditch

ANDRUS ISLAND

Georgiana Slough

S.P.R.R.

Snags

Snags

road on levee

3

2

Dead Horse I.
OVHD PWR & T CABS
AUTH CL 76 FT

1

Cable Area

Cable Area

VERT. CL AT LW 17 FT
TOWERS — 92

*A good day's cruising on Snodgrass with, top, Al Eames'
boat coming out of the channel from The Meadows;
bottom right: runabout trailing us at the top of Snodgrass;
and left, a floating home at the south end with its
boat house below, runabout in the sling
and a sailboat moored to the float.*

In summer sunlight, this dank river forest can be a place of special boating beauty. There are several narrow, overgrown canallike waterways that draw boatmen for the pleasure that comes from working through them. This one ranks at the top. The mass of leaves forms a screen, shutting out exterior noises and muffling the engine noises of other boats approaching and retreating around the shaded bends. The wakes are also dampened and do not roll with the same kind of force that comes off narrow rock or concrete-lined passageways. When observant skippers work this canyon of leafy trees, stalks and vines thoughtfully, it can become an experience of serene pastoral beauty.

On a day with time to spare in this slot, we spend a long time easing through at trolling speeds and letting other boats pass by. We drift when there is no traffic and slide out of the way when larger boats need the room to get by. The limbs and leaves of the willows and alders hang down to the water's edge and give and bend with the wash of the wakes. The overhanging greenery hides the marshy banks. It is an ideal place to explain to children how the water, constantly filtering through these muddy cells, brings nutriments from the land and growth to feeding the fish; that ecologists are stressing the need for just such swampy areas; and that whenever a concrete embankment is erected, it interrupts this process and the fish and wildlife populations suffer. Snodgrass is one of the places that feed the great fishing areas of the Delta.

Occasionally, fishermen will stick it out in this cut by holding their boats against the limbs and brambles, but these are the intrepid few who can ignore the rises and falls that come with passing hulls.

Some of the richest stands of blackberries in the world grow in this entanglement. It requires knowledge and preparation to pick them, and people familiar with the situation have several tricks for reaching the berries. They ignore the unstable banks and use ladders and special plank arrangements instead. The most sophisticated we have seen was like a cleated gangplank rigged forward and, while laid right up into the tall berry bushes, the small boat was rigged and stabilized against stumps and trunks.

Approaching boats come out of the greenery of the turns and unobtrusively disappear moments later. There is a moment of surprise when these graceful hulls appear and they have a rare kind of beauty as they move through the muted colors and strange perspectives of one's limited view.

There is always an opening, like the one at the top, for hiding out against the cool banks. Bottom: Waterskiers enjoy the open stretches along Snodgrass.

Along Snodgrass ....solitude and sunshine.

Snodgrass potpourri. Above left: Old bridges deter the big stick yachts. Right: The Mokelumne and Snodgrass Slough meet here. Below left: On the slough side of Walnut Grove is the world's largest mooring of rental houseboats. Right: An informal Richmond YC gathering gets underway.

From this slot, the entry into the restful Meadows is a sudden and dramatic experience. The exhilarating contrasts in nature's surroundings never cease to please the crews. The Meadows Slough is treated separately.

At the start of this entry is another bit of added character. It is an old railroad bridge, black and sometimes ominous in its coat of paint and creosote and, unfortunately, a solid barrier to sailboats with fixed masts. They are restricted from entering Snodgrass from the upper Sacramento, too, and the tallest must arrange in advance for a bridge tender at the Miller's Ferry swing bridge near Giusti's.

Low bridges and out-of-date bridge systems are a problem throughout much of the Delta and must be dealt with to improve the cruising range of the larger boats. Progress will not come easily and more of the sailboats and large cruisers will probably be converted to the hinged-mast arrangements that are becoming popular at some of the Southern California harbors. There is an old Delta joke that time and tide wait for no man and several tides cannot wait for the arrival of a bridge tender. But, seriously, we are not complaining about the tenders, but about the old highway system which runs through this area and must be updated to provide greater clearances where it crosses sloughs, rivers, and channels.

Crews of the larger boats often carry along one or

two smaller boats for their Delta sojourn. They secure the big boat in a familiar niche or harbor where it becomes a mother-ship to the fast, small boats. This works out very well; the small boats cover a lot of territory and can provide water skiing, fishing and transportation for sightseeing or grocery shopping trips.

Beyond the Meadows area Snodgrass rides to the north through higher, solid ground. It is a pleasant cruise in pastoral simplicity. Part of this waterway, wide and straight, is a marina for the ski boats and the exhibitionists on slats.

In the midsection of Snodgrass Slough, adjacent to the railroad bridge is a deep estuary that winds off into Lost Slough, a topic also appearing in another chapter. This is the best harbor area for the big stickers who want to be close to The Meadows and to the downstream areas of Walnut Grove and Giusti's.

In this downstream area, near the Cross Canal and the town of Locke, is a hook-shaped appendage that seldom gets any attention. It bears no name on the official charts, carries six to eight feet of water, and cuts right into the center of the big marsh that creates the largest sub-land growth on the Delta. Part of the hook is lined with interesting old cabins and tiny landings. When one can find anchorage or tie-up permission for a small boat, it is an easy walk to Locke and Walnut Grove. There is

Beautiful little coves, river-style, turn up along the slough. This one shelters a visiting houseboat.

growing enthusiasm for areas in this little slough to become boating preserves or harbors. The establishment of several landings and a limited access trail into Locke are needed. These landings would be protected from wind and currents, would provide a welcome service to boating visitors and develop business for Locke and for Walnut Grove merchants.

About one-third of the way into the Cross Channel from Snodgrass, crews can be treated to a close, straight-up view from deck or cockpit of the mighty TV antenna tower, the tallest, narrowest shaft in California.

The lower area of Snodgrass begins at Giusti's and the end of the Mokelumne River and sweeps by several of the best nonpropulsion boat houses to be seen. Their living quarters are on the second decks with their lower decks serving as parking garages for their small boats, which are lifted from the water by hoists. Walk-along strips provide fine tie-ups for visiting craft. Places to moor floating homes are scarce, but the Delta is sure to see harbor developments where structures of this kind can be accommodated.

The sweep between these boat houses and the TV tower narrows and is the location of the big Walnut Grove marina complex with marine services, houseboat rentals, an excellent sandwich restaurant and fine places to tie up.

Walnut Grove

The River Town

The architecture along Walnut Grove's quiet streets reflects the influence of the Chinese merchants. They favored overhanging balconies and shaded sidewalks.

During the sixties when the Delta was being discovered by great numbers of boating people, the favorite stopover on the middle Sacramento River was historic Walnut Grove. The landing was good, the stores were well stocked and the old hotel, which burned to the ground in 1970, was a beckoning landmark.

The levee is very high in this sector and the modern Walnut Grove has grown up along the levee road. The brown-toned hostelry at the top of the longest, steepest gangway commanded an imposing view of the river with its gentle bend.

Built in the earlier years of this century by the pioneer resident Alex Brown, the hotel was first known as the Brown and later as the Walnut Grove Hotel. On the decline and with a shrinking guest list, it was sold in 1960 to a combine with money to spend on modernization. The hotel with its fine old dark-wood bar and dining room was renamed the Boondox, a designation that caught the public fancy. Soon the entire area was being called the Boondox and legends and a mystique were being built around the nickname. This was all right in its way because it served to popularize the community and nearby stores. However, it did injustice to the fine name of Walnut Grove with its historical background. Now that the hotel's imposing presence is gone, Boondox is on the wane and the proud name of Walnut Grove seems preferred.

4

The long waterskiing runs near Walnut Grove are especially popular.

Unfortunately, the old hotel was destroyed just as a classic restoration was being planned for it by Manuel Morias, a member of the family operating nearby Giusti's Restaurant, and his associates. The group had purchased the property, and their alterations would have included a restaurant in the Delta tradition.

Boating people had lost an architectural landmark, and were also affected by the problem of maintaining the fine floating landing, only facility of its kind nearby. The local merchants cooperated with Morias in continuing the popular landing, but no plans were announced for development of the property following the fire.

Walnut Grove is a natural port for pleasure boats, because it is a waypoint in an amazing melange of popular cruising sloughs and rivers. On shore it offers sightseeing, as well as shopping, to those who walk to the sites of old Walnut Grove and Locke.

It has one standing reminder of its prominence in river shipping, which many of the other towns lack. Less than a mile up the river along the levee, and near Locke, is a long warehouse, now called The Boathouse, standing high over the water on piling. Agricultural products from the fertile hinterlands went out over the Sacramento from there and cargoes were brought in on return trips. Now that the levee roads are crowded with hopper trucks and carriers of fruit and vegetable boxes during the harvest season, the paddlewheeled hulls no longer stop at the great warehouse. But in the new age on the Delta, the drafty interior affords storage for trailerboats. They are dropped to the Sacramento by hoist, where the freight elevator once descended to the lower deck levels.

Walnut Grove's close neighbor, the Chinese community of Locke, has won popular interest and its old-world section gets most of the publicity. Because of this many people do not know that Chinese immigrants settled in Walnut Grove long before Locke existed. They became the merchants and attracted the trade of the laborers from the levees and the farms. It wasn't until 1913 that a group of Chinese who stemmed from the same province decided to build their own town, and convinced Clay Locke to let them use a portion of his orchard property.

Many who visit Locke do not also get down behind the levee to walk the old streets of Walnut Grove. The surrounding buildings are scenes right out of the old West of the river days and are well worth seeing. If these several blocks were located near or in a California city, they would be crowded and famous, but as it is, boating people receive a special bonus because they can go there and stroll in leisurely quiet. Some old-town stores are

still in business, but they are not all of Chinese ownership. The place is a photographers' and artists' bonanza and paintings and drawings of the barbershop—still operating—are on sale and reproduced in books. The main stores and services now front on the roadway that runs atop the dike. Bridges send the traffic flow in several directions to a number of island routes, some of them connected by ferries. The highway fronting Walnut Grove leads directly to Sacramento, to Stockton, and to San Francisco.

One of the joys of cruising is noticing unusual signs on places that have outlasted their founders. At Walnut Grove The Bank of Alex Brown is a name that stands out in this day of great banking chains. This bank is now in sleek new quarters but its former home still stands down the street. Thus, a fine old pioneer's name was carried forward, proving that modernization doesn't necessarily change the river area's heritage.

Efforts of steamboat owners using the Walnut Grove waterfront and Sacramento River reach were always aimed at cutting schedule time between San Francisco and Sacramento. In the early years of the 1850s they found that increased speed in riverboats and a new river course could lop off eight to nine hours between the two cities. With increased heads of steam, and the nerve to use them on snag-filled Steamboat Slough, new records were quickly set, broken and reset. The long bend was short-circuited by the through boats and so was Walnut Grove, though, of course, local freight and passenger boats continued to use this fine stretch of river. Residents were deprived of some of the century's great river steamboat races, but they were spared the agonies of numerous catastrophes that sprang from the competition between fast passenger carriers.

However, lyricism about the great white boats that adopted Steamboat Slough does not set aside Walnut Grove's continuing river glory and very definite influential position in the landside commerce of her environs.

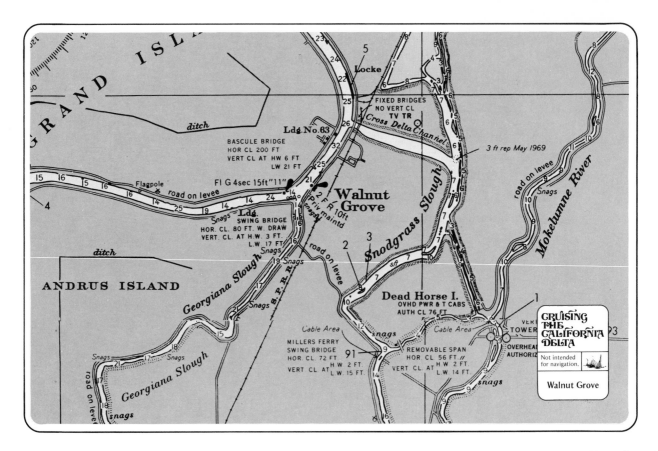

The following labels appear on the map:

GRAND ISL...

ditch

Locke

5

FIXED BRIDGES
NO VERT CL
TV TR

Cross Delta Channel

3 ft rep May 1969

Ldg. No. 63

BASCULE BRIDGE
HOR CL 200 FT
VERT CL AT HW 6 FT
LW 21 FT

road on levee

Snodgrass Slough

Mokelumne River

Flagpole   road on levee

Fl G 4sec 15ft "11"

Walnut Grove

Snags Ldg.
SWING BRIDGE
HOR. CL. 80 FT. W. DRAW
VERT. CL. AT H.W. 3 FT.
L.W. 17 FT.

ditch

ANDRUS ISLAND

Georgiana Slough

Snags

road on levee

2

3

Dead Horse I.
OVHD PWR & T CABS
AUTH CL 76 FT.

B.P.R.R.

Cable Area

MILLERS FERRY
SWING BRIDGE
HOR. CL. 72 FT.
H.W. 2 FT.
VERT. CL. AT L.W. 15 FT.

91

snags

Cable Area

REMOVABLE SPAN
HOR. CL. 56 FT.
H.W. 2 FT.
VERT. CL. AT L.W. 14 FT.

VERT
TOWER

OVERHEAD
AUTHORIZ...

snags

Georgiana Slough

Snags

road on levee

snags

CRUISING THE CALIFORNIA DELTA

Not intended for navigation.

Walnut Grove

Now after many decades have passed, the town can watch her popularity grow around the new kind of river traffic that dots the river with glistening whites, shiny chromes and the brilliant colors of pleasure boats.

Walnut Grove is in a strategic location, with ready access to the best cruising, fishing, anchoring and strenuous water sports of the western half of the Delta. A large elongated pleasure-boat harbor of simple construction is needed to service boats visiting Walnut Grove and Locke. It is a fair prediction that this will be provided through the combined resources of the two river towns.

The town's middle position on the Sacramento speaks for itself to boating families who cruise this interior river that leads out to the open sea.

Walnut Grove is the hub of some great boating and a gateway to it as well. Georgiana Slough begins to wind its attractive way south from an opening in the Sacramento only a few hundred yards downstream.

Another short and alluring river trip is ready made by staying with the old bends of the Sacramento down to Isleton and to Rio Vista.

Venerable Steamboat Slough, and the others that take off from her into out-of-the-way quiet waterways, is a reasonable distance from this hub.

The Cross Delta Canal, unfortunately limiting where its control gates work from a low, fixed overhead, nonetheless opens up an immense region for low-profile craft—The Meadows, Snodgrass Slough, several branches of the Mokelumne and many others.

An upper section of a circle is conceived for definitive ease. By tilting a compass a little to the west, and placing the point of the dividers on the chart at Walnut Grove, a mere eight-mile radius sets up all of this boating recreational paradise.

The big marina of the area is on the backside of Walnut Grove, on Snodgrass Slough below the inside terminus of the Cross Canal. Another outlying part of Walnut Grove is Giusti's Landing, near Walnut Grove Marina and at a point where the Mokelumne flows out through Snodgrass.

The story of the interesting old-town areas behind the dikes must also include the river towns of Courtland and Isleton which are not far away, although they lie in opposite directions. The survivals of river era architecture are sightseeing plums to be picked for the cost of the time that it takes to go ashore.

Though service as a sentinel is entirely outside the purpose for which it was erected, the world's tallest boating beacon stands in the farmlands back of Walnut Grove and can be seen for miles around the Delta. The singular shaft with its triangle of walkways and steelwork holds three massive TV antennas that serve all of the great valley areas.

This thin pylon extends to around 1,100 feet, more

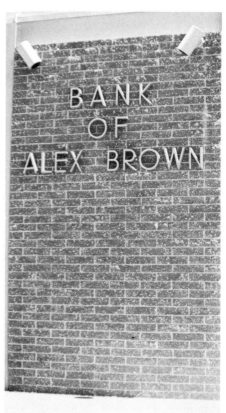

than 100 feet higher than the Eiffel Tower, for years Europe's tallest structure. The tower can be climbed from the outside, but crews are served by a centered lift. It takes 17 minutes for a one-way trip. On a clear day the State Capitol can be seen from the top.

The old West familiarized through Hollywood movies is to be found in Walnut Grove's old town. The author revisited the area in 1971, about a year after one of the movie companies had been shooting on location. Instead of building a street of false fronts for this western, they fixed up the fronts of only two of the existing structures. One became a single-story ice cream parlor and the other the two-story Cumberland Hotel. The work is remarkably deceiving and is skillfully blended into its surroundings. I was fooled and kept wondering why I didn't remember this old hotel from previous visits. I took photos from several angles to show readers of this book the kind of western town, once a Chinese center, that stretched out a few hundred yards from the Sacramento River. Unfortunately, I did not shoot from the one angle that would have exposed the movie art of construction. I was saved from embarrassment through mention of the incident to Myron Brown of the pioneer family. He set me straight when I asked him for the history of "the Cumberland Hotel." It does something for the old main street and I hope they leave it there, always, but with a plaque that tells the story.

At the landing near Walnut Grove's "Boondox," upper left, the Coast Guard talks it over with the Sheriff's patrol. Below, old piling is all that remains of the former McCarthy's Landing. The TV tower landmark and the old S.P. steamboat cargo sheds can be seen upriver. Above, right: Alex Brown pioneered Walnut Grove and the bank still bears his name.

The watery gardens of The Meadows where the trees overhang a huge field of floating lily pads in full bloom.

5 The Meadows

A Pastoral Poem

Place yourself in your cruiser on a warm summer day. You are moving through the final stretch of Snodgrass Slough toward its most celebrated vacation estuary. It has been recommended to you as the place you must visit. Your boating acquaintances have tried to describe it but any definitive image of it eludes you.

The narrowing channel approaches of 2,000 yards of swamp and brush heighten your mood of expectancy. You are reminded of the dark and murky Disneyland jungle ride without the fake alligators and elephants. The *African Queen* might be sighted around the next brushy bend. The tops of trees and brush close overhead, so only a high noon sun can filter through onto the muddy, green waters.

Suddenly the channel opens and your approaching cruiser enters a bright summer world of yachts, dinghies and small craft moving slowly on the sparkling water. There are swimmers splashing off the transom boards and floating on their plastic air mattresses. The shore is dotted with fine old shade trees.

The Meadows Slough is a separate little water channel set off entirely by itself except for its single connection with Snodgrass Slough. Once on The Meadows, you sense its remoteness from the mainstream of Delta boating. The Meadows is only 1,400 yards long but is a comparatively wide 150 yards along its course, which is as straight as a surveyor's line. It has a surprising depth of 15 feet and better. The tidal rise and fall here is not great. A low ledge of solidly packed earth edges much of the waterway, particularly on the easterly bank. On the other side, a big section slopes upward to unusually high ground for Delta country. It is from this natural, grassy terrain, without dikes, that The Meadows takes its name.

From a visit in Walnut Grove with the late Judge Milo Dye, a legendary justice in his time among the Delta residents, we learned this beautiful strip of land and water was within the vast holdings of the pioneer Clay Locke. The Lockes, the Browns and the Dyes are all Delta pioneer families and related. The Meadows has been purposely left open to visiting yachtsmen for many years so they might enjoy its waters. Clay Locke, when he was alive, enjoyed having the visiting boats, though they were far fewer in number than now. Thanks to his establishment of this hospitable policy, the fleets and their crews have been guests of the family owners of the estate ever since.

Lazy day tied up along shore at The Meadows, remote from all the action taking place to the north on Snodgrass.

Though the shoreline property is private, there is a pleasant absence of fences. No signs are posted. The yachtsman has been welcomed as a trusted guest for as many years as he and his family crew have been coming to The Meadows. The area has remained as free and open as it was in the first days of the settlers. It has the appearance of a public park and it will probably become one in time. Parks, however, are never without restrictions and rules, and something of the present freedom of The Meadows will have been lost.

Until recently, there has been no official recognition of the name, The Meadows, which stems from its shoreline surroundings. However, chart makers now recognize it as a distinct appendage to Snodgrass Slough. The 1971 issue of nautical chart 5528-SC overprints the phrase, "The Meadows Slough," alongside its course.

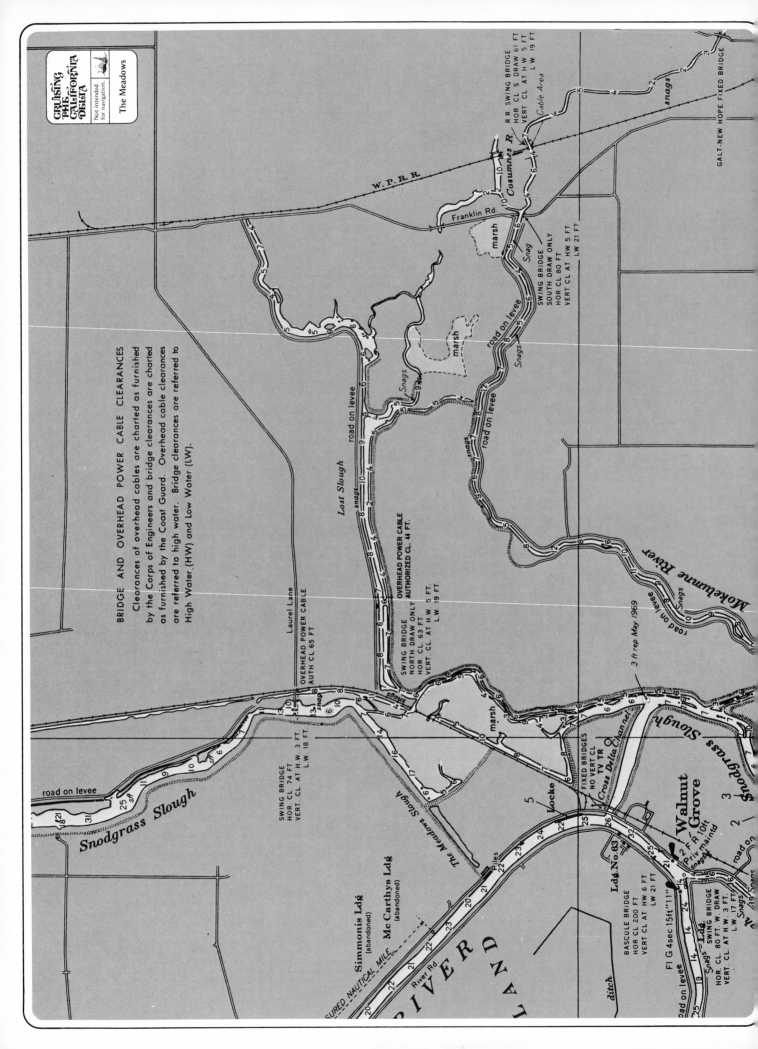

CRUISING THE CALIFORNIA DELTA

Not intended for navigation.

The Meadows

BRIDGE AND OVERHEAD POWER CABLE CLEARANCES

Clearances of overhead cables are charted as furnished by the Corps of Engineers and bridge clearances are charted as furnished by the Coast Guard. Overhead cable clearances are referred to high water. Bridge clearances are referred to High Water (HW) and Low Water (LW).

Cosumnes R.

R R SWING BRIDGE
HOR CL S DRAW 61 FT
VERT CL AT H W 5 FT
L W 19 FT

Cable Area

GALT-NEW HOPE FIXED BRIDGE

W.P.R.R.

Franklin Rd.

marsh

Snag

SWING BRIDGE
SOUTH DRAW ONLY
HOR CL 80 FT
VERT CL AT HW 5 FT
LW 21 FT

Snags

road on levee

marsh

Snags

road on levee

Lost Slough

road on levee

snags

OVERHEAD POWER CABLE
AUTHORIZED CL. 44 FT.

Laurel Lane

OVERHEAD POWER CABLE
AUTH CL 65 FT

SWING BRIDGE
NORTH DRAW ONLY
HOR CL 63 FT
VERT CL AT H.W. 5 FT.
L.W. 19 FT.

Mokelumne River

road on levee

Snags

3 ft rep May 1969

slough

SWING BRIDGE
HOR CL 74 FT
VERT CL AT H.W. 3 FT.
L.W. 18 FT.

snag

The Meadows Slough

road on levee

marsh

FIXED BRIDGES
NO VERT CL
TV TR

Cross Delta Channel

Snodgrass Slough

Snodgrass Slough

Simmonis Ldg
(abandoned)

McCarthys Ldg
(abandoned)

MEASURED NAUTICAL MILE

RIVER R O A D

River Rd.

Locke

Walnut Grove

F R 10ft
Priv maintd

Ldg. No. 63

Piles

Ldg.

snags

BASCULE BRIDGE
HOR CL 200 FT
VERT CL AT HW 6 FT
LW 21 FT

FI G 4 sec 15 ft "1"

SWING BRIDGE
HOR. CL. 80 FT. W. DRAW
VERT CL AT H.W. 3 FT.
L.W. 17 FT.

Snags

ditch

road on levee

Thousands of pleasure boats make the trek each season to the favored Meadows. The shoreline property here is private, but the yachtsmen are welcomed as trusted guests of the pioneer family owners.

The area is divided and used by the visiting boatmen in two ways. The anchoring estuary to the south, actually the section bearing the Meadows name, is rigidly self-policed by the yachtsmen who insist that wake-agitation and noise be held to a minimum. The success of this vigilance is astounding and it produces an unmistakable hush, sparkled by a low-key conversational hum and occasional laughter. People relax here. Their fun is quiet and belies the fact that dozens of cruisers and houseboats are athwart each other, held immobile in anchor-to-tree tie-downs.

To the north is a big, deep section of Snodgrass Slough, three miles in length. Here is all the action. This section is open to throaty-toned ski boats, water skiers and all who want to turn up the throttle on a runabout. There are some excellent anchoring ledges and groves of trees along the east rim of this area. Many do moor here but the disturbances from wakes is discouraging to the yachtsman bent on a peaceful, quiet anchorage.

One of our own meandering delights is to dampen our boat's propulsion to under three miles per hour, and spend several hours moving up and down the anchoring section. It is refreshing to watch boating families at ease, so thoroughly enjoying themselves. We join in their conversations carried across the transoms. We take many pictures and revel in the beauty of an anchorage estuary that compares favorably with Prideaux Haven in British Columbia and Reid Harbor in the San Juans.

If not staying overnight, we tether the bow to a willow trunk and enjoy luncheon in the shade from "the cockpit with a view." Our finale is to turn far into the hook at the end of The Meadows' course and visit the huge, natural field of floating lily pads. This tidal pond is open and usually warm. High above it, almost straight up, is the 1,100-foot TV antenna tower, about eight hundred yards away on shore. It is not offensive but it does contrast sharply with the tranquil pond of water-fed pads and leaves.

As with all cruising, the gratifications from visiting quiet inlets are many and highly personal. The Meadows deserves a special place in Delta river boating, providing another spot to anchor, unwind, and appreciate the privilege of a vacation afloat.

The Meadows is fishing, swimming, relaxing, having lunch on deck in the overhanging shade of the trees, taking a nap on an air mattress afloat on the quiet waters.

Entering The Meadows, cruisers come happily up the slough. Once in, they moor, Delta style, along the banks in the quiet anchoring estuary to the south.

Georgiana presents its visitors with classic small river scenery. There is nothing to clutter the sweeps and its broad winding curves.

6

Georgiana Slough

More Like a River

The opening into Georgiana Slough lay a few hundred feet ahead. Our bow pointed directly into it. This was early in our Delta cruising days.

We had just dropped the Walnut Grove Landing astern after shopping for supplies. It was a sunny afternoon. We expected nothing of Georgiana because no one had recommended it. Our one thought was to make harborfall at Korth's grand layout at the mouth of the Mokelumne. The chart showed that this was the shortest way to get there.

Until then we had passed up Georgiana only because we had had no occasion to use it. But now I pulled up short on the throttle. Here, directly before us, was the classic river scene, the kind we had seen many times on the smaller rivers of the Northwest. It had a slow velocity look to it, an interesting bridge, a cluster of floats and small work boats, dolphins and fender pilings and stands of willows. A photographer could spend a lot of time on this scene, photographing it from every angle, in every kind of light.

Since that first time we have returned often. A brisk run through Georgiana has always been a pleasure. There are no tule islands to clutter the sweeps. The course is clearly defined. The broad, winding curves are a delight.

We have found the entire length attractive, with the upper half of the slough more wooded than the rest. We have particularly enjoyed its cooling qualities late in the afternoon of a warm day. Georgiana is one of those waterways that may best be enjoyed in a fast run. We like to take Georgiana from north to south. The warmth of the day cools just enough. The wake lays in fold on fold. The green shadows contrast the hot sky and the waning sun. We have also enjoyed cruising it northward in the morning, when it has a different effect.

Georgiana also has a two-mile-long hairpin bend, the longest of its type in the Delta. In its center is an island with an inner harbor. This harbor is scheduled for a big marina, restaurant and resort area, which will be a fine addition to Delta boating.

*The entrance to Georgiana Slough
from the Sacramento. Georgiana is a favorite
shortcut between the cities of Sacramento and Stockton.*

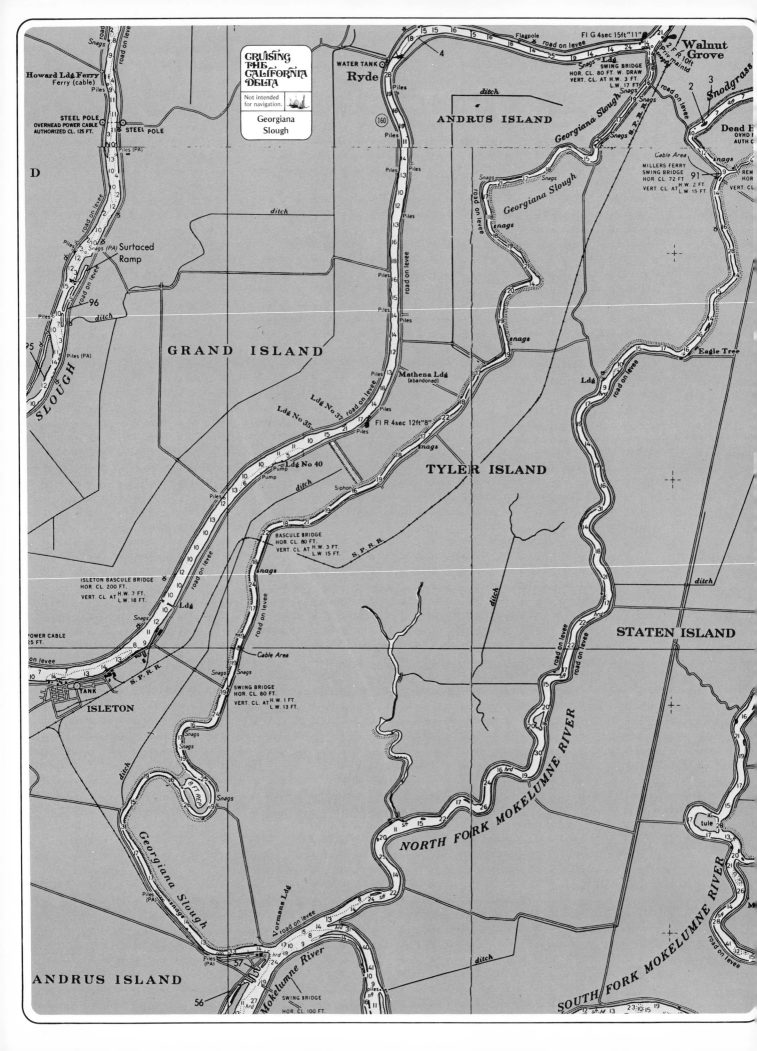

Georgiana is a shortcut between Stockton and Sacramento but the steamboats did not use it often. There were many snags and, in places, it was too shallow for the larger boats. The hairpin bend might also have been a deterrent.

For some reason, this slough does not get much of the houseboat travel that one sees everywhere else.

Rows of pilings from abandoned farm landings serving Andrus and Tyler islands are signs of other days.

As late as the 1920s, many of these landings were still served by the sternwheeler *Neponset No. 2.* But one day she punched the limb of a big snag through her planks and went to the bottom. Money was short and the owners abandoned her on the spot. So, ironically, an overworked government snag boat, which had not been able to keep the river free of old trees, was given the job of removing the *Neponset* from the channel. She was ripped apart by the snagging crews and heaped on the levee shore. Much of her is reported to have been used for firewood.

Georgiana drops into the Mokelumne just above the highway bridge that leads to Rio Vista. The B & W Boat Resort is nearby and on the point is a large, grassy park with a big sandy beach. This is a very popular beach with the water skiers.

I have wondered about the name of this slough. There was a famous steamboat called *Georgiana,* but I have never been able to learn whether she was connected with the slough. However, this is one of our favorite trips and this river does save cruisers from having to take the long way around between Stockton and Sacramento.

An overcast day along Georgiana. Aboard the Yankee K. *at top, Len Atwood takes the helm. Below: Old clay jugs, brought over by the Chinese, may still be uncovered in the levee mud of the Delta.*

The Chinese Built Locke

The first time we saw Locke a party of us were trudging in the back way from a slough that curls off Snodgrass Slough. We crossed a field standing high with summer weeds and grass and approached an ancient two-story bunkhouse that housed a number of elderly Chinese men. Their lives would end before they could return to their homeland. Their faces were cracked and weathered from years of levee building and farm work—as cracked and weathered as the unpainted clapboard siding of their makeshift residence.

My efforts to edge those on the porch into poses for my camera failed. These immigrants and sons of immigrants are cautious and reticent. Only dozing cats stayed in sight when I tried to take pictures.

Many tales of Locke's bustling days piqued our expectations as we turned into the narrow main business block where Locke's few establishments continue to operate. With one long look, we stepped back 45 years into a western town of a kind we had never known. There is only one Locke. It is different from the other "wooden towns" of the same period throughout the coastal northwest.

A leisurely stroll through old Locke is always a pleasure for visiting yachtsmen. Those who have not seen its architecture may soon regret delaying the trip. It may not remain as it is unless there is a concerted public effort to preserve its historic features. Locke is a unique Delta anachronism. A series of outdoor plaques should be erected tracing its origins and the histories of individual buildings in the same way that traditional southern cities mark buildings they have preserved and restored. So far no one has started such a movement for Locke, and it is fading. The original building fronts still stand but most of the activity within them has ceased.

In early days Locke was a gathering place for the Chinese who were working on the levees and the farms. They could stave off loneliness by being among others speaking their native language. The chief entertainments were the gambling games—the "wide open" activities that were carried on before and after prohibition—and the offerings of the Oriental Star Theater. The merchants who sold food and supplies and contracted for the labor gangs headquartered at Locke.

The Chinese founders of the town built Locke around one main street of stores with their living quarters upstairs. Each building had a second-story porch or balcony, which extended out over the sidewalk. These up-

The entry to the famous old Star Theater in Locke where, from 1913 to the mid-twenties, the Chinese settlers staged their plays and entertainments.

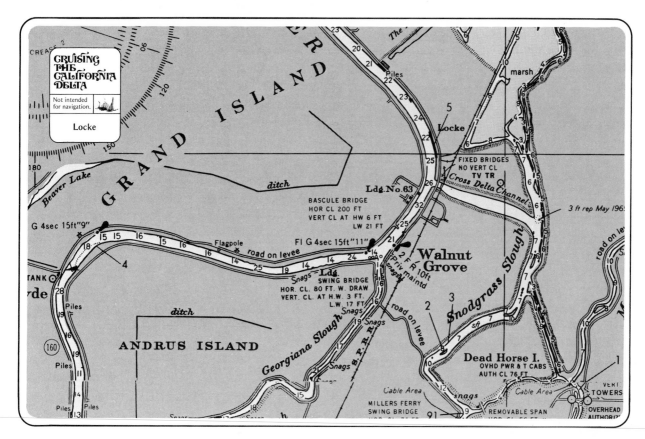

stairs porches provided families with a place to sit outside and protected the street-level sitters and walkers from the heat of the summer and the wet of the winter. These sidewalks, roofed by the upstairs porches from one end to the other, became Northern California's earliest shopping mall, long before the term was coined.

Locke's interesting main street is on the flat behind the levee and below the level of the nearby Sacramento River. There are also businesses along the levee road, but Locke is remembered for this one historic street. It is sometimes called "The Street of Tales," a place around which many stories have grown up, some of them humorous, some unlikely. Unfortunately, few have been recorded.

One establishment is still popular with yachtsmen today. Al's Place has built a reputation as a bar and steak restaurant that reaches far and wide, always under the nickname of "Al, the Wop's." In Delta conversation, it has been slurred into a familiar "Alawop's." It is a Delta institution.

Al, it is generally admitted, became associated with this Chinese business section during bootlegging days. He later built the restaurant and it has been maintained and operated in the old tradition since his death. So the only widely known old restaurant in Locke is not Chinese but Italian.

My second try at photographing Locke was as futile as my first, but was remarkable in one way. While the rest of the invaders from the cockpits were shopping, I was trying to get a wide-angle picture down the length of the main street that is little more than two autos wide. I worked my light meter from beneath my arm and set my lens by reaching down into the camera bag behind a post. With everything set, I quickly sneaked the camera up to eye level and clicked the shutter. I obtained a good photo of the street but the benches are bare where the old men had been sleeping in the warmth. The photo shows just one pair of legs vanishing through a nearby doorway. The visitor must be prepared for a distrust of anyone who takes pictures.

*Locke, the Delta's Chinatown, with its
narrow streets and its overhanging porches.*

There are more misconceptions about the establishment of Locke than there are facts in print. It is not very old. Walnut Grove came first, as was mentioned earlier, and had its own Chinatown. The town burned down and was rebuilt several times. After one such fire in 1914, some of the Chinese moved out and built the new town on property which Clay Locke had been cultivating as a pear orchard.

Locke is the only town in America actually built by Chinese. It is remarkable that they even built Locke because, in those days, they could not own property. Today, the buildings are still on the Locke estate.

Myron Brown, a Walnut Grove insurance executive and business man, who has family connections with the Lockes, says that he has always understood that the Walnut Grove Chinese had some form of tong organization and the two groups in town had separated along these lines.

Ping Lee, an erudite second-generation merchant who owns Big Store, the grocery and meat market near The Bank of Alex Brown, comments that his father said that the split was largely a matter of dialects. "The Chinese people in Walnut Grove spoke two dialects because they were from two districts, one the Chung-san (or Heuong-shan) and the other the Toy-shan, he explained. "They naturally could converse better with people from their district so when Walnut Grove burned to the ground the Chung-sans moved up to the new site."

Continuing his reminiscences, Ping Lee said: "My father died in 1970 at the age of 97, my mother ten years earlier. (She came over in 1914.) And I have tried to get my facts of the early life here the best that I can from conversations with my father and from knowing many of the other people. It is hard to be always sure of facts and so little is written down.

"The movement of Chinese as levee builders began in the 1860s. They came from railroad building, from gold digging and from San Francisco, the hub for the Chinese. My father came to Walnut Grove from San Francisco in 1897. Chinatown was established, but earlier it had been a half-mile down river. There is a Chinese graveyard near the first site, but very few markers are left.

"After three fires, what now stands as Walnut Grove's China section was built since 1937. The old one was like a town on a wharf, built ten feet above the ground and above the winter flooding. In the winter the people had to park their buggies on higher ground down by the theater and walk on little paths. My dad was a farm worker, met Alex Brown and became his cook. Later, he worked at the Walnut Grove Hotel. Then he went into business in Walnut Grove, a busy Chinese community. He sold merchandise and also contracted labor for the farms. Everyone wanted to make money and go back to China.

"Walnut Grove was alive with stores, homes, and gambling houses. Gambling was wide open, tolerated. Then the fire came. My father and four other merchants went to the Locke estates, near the Southern Pacific wharf, where there were two houses, one a restaurant and one a little hotel. These buildings stand today. The site was selected because Mr. Locke was willing to pull out the pear trees and let Chinatown get started. In those days the only trade was with the Chinese. It was later that Americans came to shop.

"In those early days, one in twenty of the Chinese men had a family. Signs on the store fronts would advertise for labor on the farms. The men worked six days and wanted one in town to eat with their people, gamble a little and relax. When the boss said, "Everyone in the buggy, we're going back to camp," those who were working were gone for a week.

"The Oriental Star Theater staged Chinese plays with traveling professional troupes. These were few, and sometimes amateurs put on the shows. Chinese movies were sometimes shown, too. There were no Americans in the audiences. Later, the theater building was turned into a rooming house.

"In its best days there were a half dozen grocery stores, a bakery, four restaurants, fish markets, and gambling houses. I hear the talk of prostitution, too, but these were white people, operating in a river town as they did everywhere.

"Al came along in 1932 and bought the building from me. It had been my father's. In Locke he had built up eight stores, more than anyone else. These burned. Then he built five more in Locke. He was prosperous among the merchants.

"It was always the desire to have one's body, after death, returned to the old country. There are many tales about this. I do know many were buried in San Francisco and Delta graveyards and arrangements were made to ship the bones to China many years later.

"The younger people don't stay here today. I left but came back because this was my father's home and I am glad I did. Around here there are more Chinese over 65 years old than under it. There are 15 people over 80 years old. Locke has the most Chinese families among the little Delta towns, about 20 families, besides the single men."

Ping Lee is fifty now. Here we have only barely touched on some of the facts and stories he has uncovered in his effort to trace the history of his people in the Delta. He speaks with marvelous fluency, enthusiasm and pride. Ping Lee does the cooking when entertaining at home, and is a specialist in true Cantonese cookery.

The late Erle Stanley Gardner discovered the California Delta in his later years and made many friends there. In his 1967 book, *Gypsy Days on the Delta*, Gardner mentions Grandfather King and George Marr, and his own pleasure at shopping at their market. He delighted in purchasing their Chinese oyster sauce, pickled scallions, special cheeses and especially the bean cake cheese. The fine modern market, operated by many generations of the Marr and King families, still serves the area today.

There are Chinese-operated restaurants along the levee road. Despite the lack of landings, the old Southern Pacific Railroad warehouse, one of the few of its kind standing, is still used as The Boat House. As mentioned in the chapter on Walnut Grove, it houses trailer-borne pleasure boats and gently drops them down 30 feet into the Sacramento with a special sling and hoist arrangement.

Locke is well worth a visit, particularly if the skipper and his family have the time to go ashore and wander through the old town.

At Locke, the sight of a camera sends the elderly Chinese men heading for the doorways.

The Mokelumne

River with a Big Loop

Boats can only use about forty miles of the Mokelumne River, including its two widely divided forks. But the deep forks are a main brace for boating for a big central area above the San Joaquin River and east of the long, snaking Sacramento.

In the usual scheme of things, the two forks of a river, once their channels have diverged, empty at different points. But the Mokelumne is unusual in this regard. Its North Fork and South Fork run in a big loop, rejoining just five miles from the mouth and flowing as one through an S-curve and into the San Joaquin.

This river is very convenient for pleasure-boat skippers. The two forks are in constant use because they lead to many other connections with the whole interlocking system of waterways in the upper central region.

As with many other Northern California rivers that begin high in the Sierra Nevada, the Mokelumne was named for an Indian tribe. Muk-kel was the name of its main village and "umne" means "the people of." It is pronounced mu-col'-umne with the first *u* very soft.

It is difficult to explain the names of its two forks. The North Fork is on the west side running vertically with the compass rose and one would expect to call it the west fork. The South Fork is on the east side, running generally parallel to its sister fork, until it almost reaches the San Joaquin. Then it flows east to west to tie the loop, partly supporting its claims to the "southerly" designation. The loop is shaped like a rubber band lying on the chart table.

The busiest stretch on the river. Willow Berm Marina is in the background.

8

Most of the people using the Mokelumne pay little attention to its main course above the divided forks. They generally think that it ends somewhere in the interior around the dry Lodi area. Glances at the charts appear to substantiate this.

But people who are familiar with the high country know a different Mokelumne, an exciting one. It starts with three branches that merge, trickling and tumbling out of vast canyons high in the mountains not far from the Nevada State line. One of these branches is only 40 miles from Lake Tahoe and another is about 60 miles from Yosemite Valley. These are beautiful areas of high rugged land, vastly different from the boating areas of the Mokelumne. John C. Fremont and Kit Carson tramped this high country and undoubtedly crossed these little branches many times as they established the Alpine Highway trail.

Knowing that the river comes clear and clean out of country of such exceptional beauty forces a healthy contemplation of our often too casual treatment of our lowland waters.

The development of the upper North Fork for water power dates from the Gold Rush days of the middle nineteenth century. These mountain waters were brought into flumes and ditches for placer mining and quartz operations. Later they became sources for the great hydroelectric systems of the West. They helped remove an estimated $300 million in gold and, regrettably, filled in river channels with the by-products of hydraulic mining. The gold camps that grew up near these waters entered into the writings of Bret Harte and Samuel Clemens and the accounts woven around the infamous Black Bart.

But today's values must be reckoned also. Water is stored, electricity generated, floods are controlled, lowlands made safe and boating is benefited by a system of eight reservoirs storing a half-million acre feet of the Mokelumne's pure water. The Salt Springs Reservoir in the watershed is one of the most important pure water sources and is also a place of rare wilderness beauty, a great rock gorge with fine stands of evergreens. The reservoir facility has not spoiled the beauty of the terrain.

The Mokelumne has forks at either end, each with its own great importance to California. The two lower branches are known to untold numbers of boating people and are quite different from each other. The cross-route portion of the South Fork opens into interesting boating territory near the old river station of Terminous. From that point, the fork swings to the north. There are good depths part of the way up, but the northerly track becomes narrow and its depths become inconsistent as one "works up hill." It is generally avoided by the big boats whose skippers have many other routes from which to choose.

Two views of the B&W Harbor on the Mokelumne. The surrounding grounds of this busy river facility are rich in lawn and trees ... and beautifully maintained.

However, this section is a delight for the small cruiser people all the way to New Hope Landing. It is a busy and exciting playground for those with open boats in which the skipper does not have to squint constantly out of a bright sun into a depthsounder dial to read the river's shifting mudbars and check that deeper riffs are not harboring snags. An occasional large cruiser is run up to New Hope as a lark, but for clearing the bars the water must be adequate. Also, for clearing the two fixed-height bridges the cruiser's upper deck must not be too high. Though the spans are removable, this is done only in very special cases. So, for most of the large cruisers and sailboats this is a "deadend street," and there is no advantage to the shortcut to Snodgrass Slough. The South Fork above Terminous is dotted with skeeter boats and every kind of modern, low-profile craft. There are numerous sloping beaches of river sand, speed and ski-ways, good courses for cruising and many inviting places for the family crew to wade, swim and picnic.

New Hope Landing is situated between the two bridges near the old Walnut Grove road and is very popular. There are long floats and good fuel facilities, a good cafe and snack bar. It is generally a fine place for visiting small boats and pontoon houseboats. On summer weekends, it is the busiest place on the Delta.

For at least eight months of the year, pleasure boats churn the upper South Fork.

The Yankee K. *runs the channel on her way to a Spindrift Yacht Club cruise. The berm in the background is all that is left of Central City.*

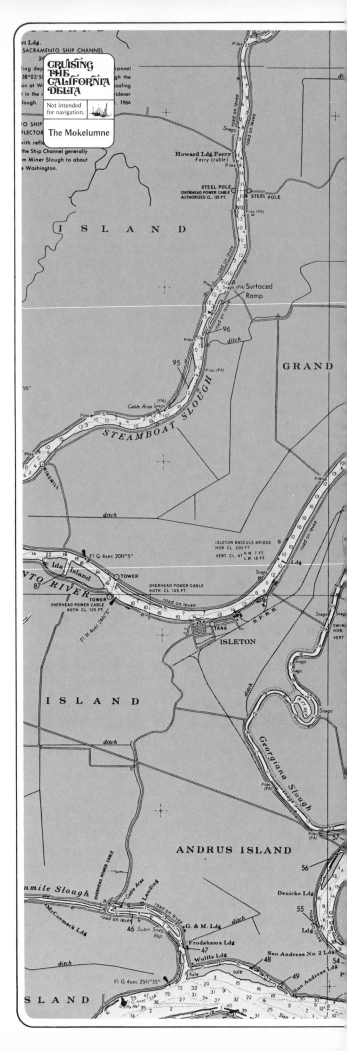

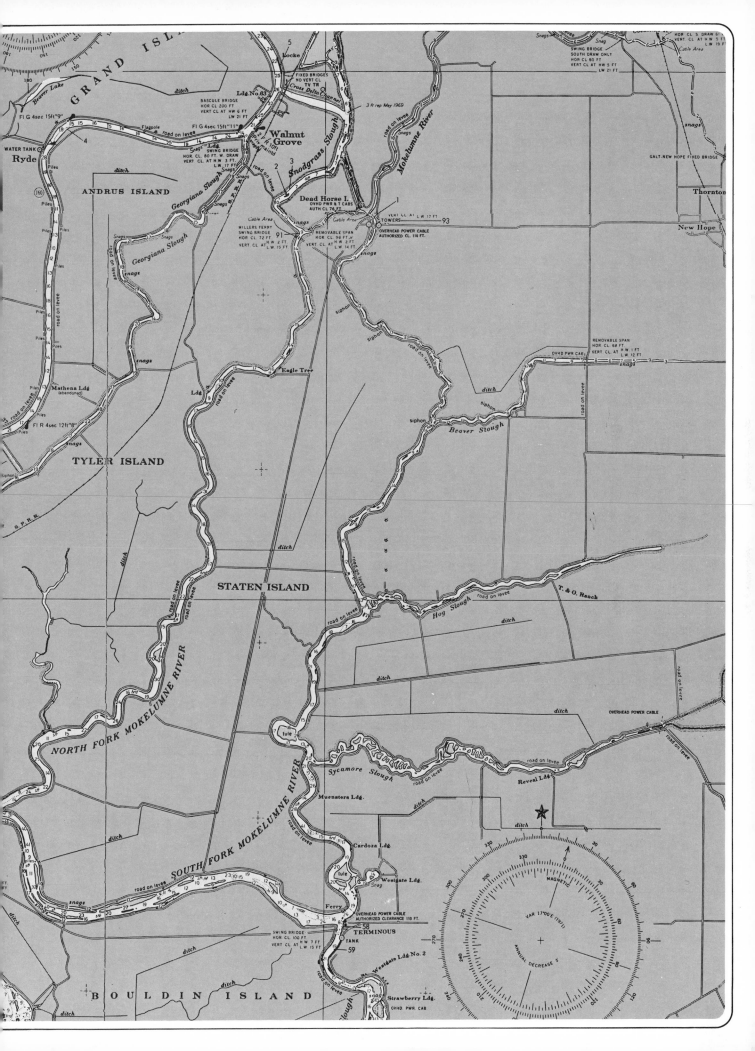

The old piling, above, provides flower pots along the Mokelumne. Bottom, left: A Delta visitor uses one of the many good marina launching ramps. Right: A South Fork beach.

The river is keenly attuned to the boating people. A bridge tender (top) looks down on a busy Mokelumne. Pacific Gypsy (center) is steel-hulled and one of the Delta's largest regulars. Here she is bow-into her home port, a narrow slot among the willows. Korth's Pirates Lair Marina (bottom) provides boaters a fine protected harbor and excellent services.

There are three little sloughs branching to the east from this fork—Sycamore, Hog and Beaver. They offer little to the main boating fare. Beaver is the only one whose depths are listed on the Coast and Geodetic Survey Chart. The first two are for light craft and those who want to putter around for a few miles. These streams will occasionally widen and grow a tule island or two in the middle. These permit several courses around them and broad, arcing turns, or even a full circle if the skipper chooses. The South Fork has two islands, one at the Sycamore offshoot and the other near Terminous. In some ways these are of no consequence, but they can break the monotony of a straight run, often provide off-course day anchorages.

The cross section of the South Fork ends at Terminous in the east and opposite Georgiana Slough in the west. There the open junction of four river bodies creates a soft cross and a big, deep reach. Some have said the thing looks like an octopus. This piece of the river flows west for five miles and is fine for open cruising. It has a number of long tule islands close to the upper bank. Anchoring places can be found if care is taken. This stretch parallels the famous Potato Slough, which is much wider and has islands which create better anchorages for the larger boats.

The Mokelumne's waters come together again in a five-mile run to the broadened San Joaquin River which is an open cruising and fishing ticket to everywhere. This run is the center of the Delta, separating Andrus and Bouldin Islands and dumping its silt into San Andreas Shoal. During the long boating season, no daytime moment passes in which the sun does not reflect off pleasure boats and rented houseboats on the move, some bound in, some out. The constant movement is fascinating. The makeup of the fleet is an illuminating cross section of many size categories, with quality running generally very high.

*A Bertram (top) lays a wake headed down the Moke-
lumne. Little tule ridges create side waterways. This one
(bottom photo) hides a passing pontoon houseboat.*

In their use of the Mokelumne River, these peripatetic fleets are attracted to a string of fine marina harbors and service centers. This boating harbor row is grouped all along the Andrus Island shoreline. These centers stand high in the memories of visiting boaters because they have never seen anything similar in their home ports. The setting is river wilderness. The marina harbors are warm and protected. Visitors' floats are long and people are accommodating. The covered stalls shelter flotillas of fine resident boats. There is a mixture of planted trees, green lawns, little restaurants and spas, people enjoying their holidays in the cockpits and on the decks. It is a happy water carnival.

The owners of the resident boats come from all over Northern California with a few living year-round in the area. Levee roads connect the groups of marine establishments with each other and with the towns of Rio Vista, Isleton, Walnut Grove, Antioch and Stockton.

In their loose affinity with each other, offering ports and service equally to their regulars and to visitors, these places have created a kind of social order. Friendships develop. Families cruise their boats together. There is a noticeable pride and affection for the area, a kind of personal yacht club feeling.

These places are a part of the new economy of the Delta. They occupy property that once held the steamboat landings of Gibson, Pedro, San Andreas and Denicke.

This series of neighboring marinas begins on the San Joaquin behind a very long tule island which creates a natural breakwater and set of entrance channels. Bruno's Yacht Harbor is here, with covered moorings and many services. Several seasonal moorings are nearby for sailboats needing plenty of water under their keels and plenty of sky room for their masts.

Popular Spindrift Marina is also behind this protecting island, offering fuel services, yacht sales, mooring, engine and electrical services and a dinner restaurant that is open on key days of the week. The Spindrift Yacht Club has its home here.

From Spindrift Marina, it is a few miles around to the wide mouth of the Mokelumne River and the stone breakwater protecting Korth's Pirate Lair Marina from the swells of river traffic and currents. Korth's has permanent moorings, guest floats and fuel services, yacht sales, launching facilities for small boats, a busy coffee shop and a park that blends native trees and palm trees in California fashion.

Central City, near the mouth of the Mokelumne opposite Moore's present Riverboat installation, a village of Chinese inhabitants, went down in one of the floods of the thirties. Some buildings were hauled away on barges. The top photograph, from the Charles K. Davis collection, shows the salvage work in progress. Below, left: Another Davis collection flood photo— a closeup as the old house begins to lean into the river.

Above: Beach scene on a narrow upper reach of the South Fork. Below: Perrys, a large marina of covered berths, also provides repairs with elevator-lift service.

*The Mokelumne's marina row is a Delta
Main Street for yachtsmen. Top: View of Bruno's
several locations for large sailboats that
are kept on the Delta in the summer. Bottom: Weekending
yacht crews gather at Harry Schilling's Spindrift Marina.*

Moore's Yacht Harbor has a limited marina, is connected to the fine Delta Boat Works and its large elevator boat lifts, but is really known for its Riverboat Restaurant. The Riverboat does more drop-in-by-water business than any other place on the Delta.

Willow Berm Marina, abutting Moore's, is one of the newest and largest covered mooring and service complexes in Northern California.

Within the wide crescent of the lower Mokelumne there are several smaller marinas with fuel, launching and dry storage facilities, and eating counters. The Lighthouse is one of these.

At the upper end of this string of marinas, the big highway bridge crosses the Mokelumne, joining the levee road which connects the complexes with each other and the outside world. Perry's Boat Harbor is big, with covered moorings, repairs, and fuel services. Perry's specializes in haulouts for propeller and shaft work. This is where The Perry Nut, an electrolysis preventer mounting for the top of the propeller shaft, is manufactured.

Closing this long marina row is the B & W Resort, a fine combination of woods, large grassy plots, a mooring harbor, cottages, guest floats and fuel service, excellent launching ramps and a refreshment building. It is a quiet harbor in a sylvan setting. It is also the headquarters for the Mokelumne Yacht Club.

Mokelumne moods. Top: The beach at B&W Point where they gather for sun bathing, swimming and water-skiing. Center: Bog-bumping and fishing. Bottom: From the Mokelumne into the San Joaquin in the early evening.

The upper Mokelumne reaches are cool and shaded, among the very best. A cruiser, above, is almost hidden among the tree branches.

The Upper Mokelumne

The main stream of the Mokelumne River winds across flat country to a point near Deadhorse Island, about two miles inland from Walnut Grove, where it flows into its two big branches. Ignoring the official chart designations of North Fork Mokelumne River and South Fork Mokelumne River, skippers and residents of the area usually refer to both source and branches as "the Mokelumne." Increasing the chance of confusion is the fact that these very supple streams in the lowlands, among the levees, are separate from the three forks of the Mokelumne that come down through 4,000-foot canyons in Alpine County.

For clarity in conversation and writing, we call the navigable section above New Hope Landing "the Upper Mokelumne." It is without official sanction but this designation makes geographic sense. People pick it up quickly and it saves a lot of explaining.

This so-called Upper Mokelumne is a river of gentle surfaces. It possesses the prettiest curving reaches in these wonderful miles of cruising waterways. Its beauty is enhanced by great stands of cottonwoods, willows, sycamores and occasional oaks and maples, many of them very old. Curving waters and heavy growth create privacy—or at least semiprivacy. As we have said before, boating explorers tend to stay in the lower regions and ignore the five to eight navigable miles of the Upper Mokelumne.

It is true navigation is somewhat restricted after the first several miles. There are occasional snags and a slight rise in the riffles. But small boats have no problems, as we pointed out in the previous chapter. It would be a fair generalization that powerboats up to 30 feet and the smaller houseboats have a negotiable eight miles, with many little tie-in places, if skipper and crew exercise reasonable caution.

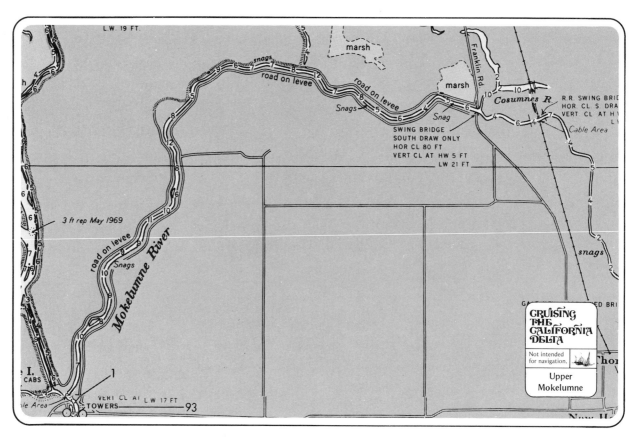

This houseboat was marooned with a dead battery. We supplied the cable jumpers and she got underway.

Some intrepid skippers, with shallow-draft boats and the desire for a lark on the Mokelumne when it is at its seasonal high, travel the entire 18 miles to interior Woodbridge and to points near the dam forming Smith Lake (a lovely park that has its own runabout fleet on the upper side of the dam). But most boats on the Delta are concerned primarily with the first eight miles of river above its two-fork junction. How far they go beyond the two bridges near the Cosumnes River entry is a matter of the skipper's choice and his knowledge of the general lay of the riverbed in relation to the depth of the water.

Any run made today is inconsequential when compared to the struggle that took place more than a hundred years ago when river freighting came to the Mokelumne—briefly and not very successfully. Few of our yachting-cap river pilots are aware that these bends and wooded canyons once vibrated to the shish-shush of moving pistons on steamers with irregular schedules.

One of the busiest landings on the Delta is at New Hope (top). The bottom photo shows New Hope's houseboat row. But inland from this bustle, the beautiful upper Mokelumne is strangely free of traffic.

Crayfishing with traps (top) is a regular river pastime. So are pontoon houseboats (center). Sea-Niles (bottom) is moored near the Cosumnes River.

There were no junks on the Delta when they built the levees. Now this one enjoys the beauty the Chinese helped create.

Undoubtedly, with all the problems attending the attempt to conquer the Mokelumne and establish transportation to the inland, there was plenty of loud shouting of commands from captains and pilots down to the deckhands who swung the leads into the shallows. Old accounts indicate it was not easy to read the river, swing the hulls around some of the turns and avoid the snags that could punch a hole in the planking. The river depths and situations were different in those days. They were affected by unbridled water flows, by silt and rocks and even by encroaching dregs from placer mining. The levees were different, too, and it is hard for us today to visualize the earlier Mokelumne. Old records indicate it was never intended to be a navigable river for small freight boats—at least not for long distances on consistent schedules.

However, a pioneering Dr. Locke did not see it that way. In 1862 he chartered a 110-foot freighter and gave instructions to the captain that all encumbrances of banks and water were to be overcome. The steamer was to reach Lockeford and substantiate the claim that the town had freight and passenger service. The trip was slow and the boat was tied up to trees overnight on several occasions. In addition, there was Mr. Wood of Woodbridge to be reckoned with. It seems that he was able to use various forms of persuasion with the steamboat captain and Dr. Locke's *Fanny Ann* was detained at Woodbridge.

This had the effect of establishing the importance of riverboat service to the growth of one town over the other and the fight was on. Apparently Dr. Locke did not give up easily. He leased other steamers and occasional service did exist all the way up the river to Lockeford. He formed the Mokelumne River Navigation Company and carried on difficult snag-clearing operations. His tenacity and the money he spent almost created an inland port. However, there were too many problems. The Civil War was at its height and, whether or not this influenced his decision, transportation service on the inland section of the Mokelumne ceased. Now this beautiful stretch is available to the pleasure boats.

The bottoms near the stream are fertile. Quaint old ranch buildings add to the sense of remoteness. The river grows narrow as we go upstream. The trees become dominant. There are only occasional short open stretches. The rest is a deep cover of green.

Near the entry to the Cosumnes River is a ledge for camping with a water depth that permits a houseboat to be taken right up to the trees. Clusters of wild bush and huge trees create spring temperatures even during the valley's summer heat. This spot was the late Erle Stanley Gardner's Shangri-la. He would cook the fish he caught over an open fire and stay for several days at a time. His Delta journals tell of his hopes to settle there.

*Upper Mokelumne albums will have
bridges crossing the old narrows; wakes
laid among the tangles as one winds down the
reaches and view after view of this prettiest of rivers.*

The return journey downstream is also delightful. The turns are long and graceful. The snags are not too dangerous and are no hazard to a watchful skipper. We usually stop several times to hold the boat under big trees and take refreshment.

During our own cruising seasons, our association with this scenic section of the upper Mokelumne came through casual discovery. Its boating pleasures, which we rate very high in terms of river boating, had never been extolled to us. Whenever discoveries like this are made, they bring a rewarding sense of personal ownership and identification with a particular area.

Lost Slough branches off from Snodgrass and begins with a deep harbor surrounded by a low river forest. It then opens out into two long canals leading through open meadow country. Lost Slough is well worth the diversion from the boatman's journey up Snodgrass.

It is generally agreed there are not a great many different kinds of enjoyment within the limitations of cruising a small boat in a confined area. Certainly there is not the choice that is open to the owners of the large crafts capable of traveling great distances to places of exotic scenery or historic import.

However, many captains of large personal yachts have learned that morning trips in the dinghy, that modern equivalent of the longboat, are stimulating. There is a special feeling about being very close to the water with your feet, in fact, below the waterline. There is challenge and adventure in seeking what lies out yonder and conducting such exploration intimately, from the water's own level.

We Found Lost Slough

*Lost Slough provides an estuary
straight enough for eight-oar crew racing.*

10

It was this way for us with Lost Slough. While to us it had never been lost, we simply had never looked for it nor heard of it. Local charts treat it lightly if at all. We had glanced into the short leg of its opening, admiring the beauty of the dense growth along its course, but we had thought it a deadend branch of Snodgrass Slough.

All this changed on a fortunate day when a friend, who knows every turn and tree from a lifetime around the Delta waterways, said, "Come on. We'll take the 19-foot utility and I'll show you one of my favorites and why I like it." Now we have added it to our own list of Delta side-trip favorites.

Lost is a minor slough in the grand scheme of Delta cruising. It is about three and a half miles long and runs a moderate course to the north, the top slough in the middle alley of the Delta. Lost Slough starts from the big marsh in the middle section of Snodgrass and makes one short move up before its 90° turn out through higher country on the side of Snodgrass opposite The Mead-

ows. Lost Slough's endings finger out in several directions not far from the Mokelumne and Cosumnes rivers through the farm fields extending down from the Sacramento area. The scenery is more open.

At its start, Lost Slough is a large, dark harbor with waters the same murky tones of green one sees in the depths of its parent stream, Snodgrass. The entrance to Lost Slough is near the railroad bridge and so it is popular with the sailboats. They can't clear for The Meadows so they drop off here to anchor and to latch their spring lines onto a friendly tree. This is an excellent place for sailboat anchorage. At its big turn, the stream widens into a large crescent with quiet mooring spots for many boats. It is not unusual for families to stay here for long vacations while the skippers commute to the cities for business appointments and an occasional day at the office. Most skippers bring in auxiliary runabouts making it easy to get around. This Lost Slough harbor is a favorite of members of the Richmond Yacht Club.

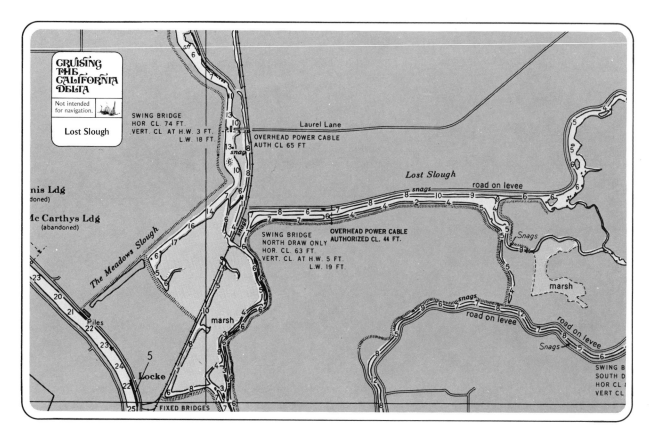

*Lost Slough scenery. The marine gardens of
Lost Slough are mounded with thousands of lily pads. This is also a
slough of curving sweeps and bends, deep growth
at its beginnings, tule islands forming its
straight-as-an-arrow twin courses.*

*A schooner
rests in a slough hole.*

From the big turn, the area quickly opens up. The official depths remain surprisingly good. The course on each side of the slough is long and almost surveyor straight. The view down its reach, as it stretches between the tule islands on one side and the willows on the levees on the other, has the appearance of a great, natural estuary of a mall.

The dredging, done to build up the dikes, has increased Lost Slough's boating charms by deepening the straightaways and leaving the long, thin tule islands up the middle. The two attractive courses hardly react to the light tidal movements and would be excellent places for eight-oar crew racing.

Lost Slough's water seems clearer and bluer than in many other parts of the Delta. Lovely farmland comes right down to the edges. There is a depth six to nine feet along most of its three and a half miles. The course seems short but this amounts to considerably more mileage when one cruises each side of the screening tule islands and around some of the forks at the end. These center berms or "islands" are each so long that, in effect, two cruising sloughs have been created. Near the end the water fans out into an attractive wide lake.

The entire trip, though short, calls for many stops and a lot of loafing afloat while enjoying the pastoral scenery.

There are several gorgeous stands of water lilies in the wide area. The fields of these floating flowers with their thick, green leaves are probably as striking as any in the West and create marine garden atmosphere for the enjoyment of the exploring yachtsmen.

Cruisaday families, curious to see what is at the other end of a slough, will enjoy taking time from their main exploration of Snodgrass to find Lost Slough.

The banks of Steamboat have been drawing yachts to their trees for many years.

Steamboat Slough

The River Mansion Story

Steamboat Slough is actually more a big segment of the Sacramento River than it is a slough. This offshoot of the Sacramento was, as its name suggests, the original route of the old paddlewheelers. The race course of the audacious river captains has now become the quiet waterway of the cruising pleasure boaters.

In 1947, while editing *Pacific Motor Boat,* SEA magazine's predecessor, I accepted an article written by a Northern California East Bay yachtsman. He described the tranquil Delta vacation life enjoyed by owners of large sailboats and cruisers. These people had established a friendly summer colony afloat, on the west bank of Steamboat Slough's north end in the shade of the towering willows and cottonwoods. I became intrigued with the idea of lines set against levee tree trunks and yachts anchored against river currents. The author's photos showed the use of small auxiliary boats for exploring the peaceful, inviting Delta scenery. Right then I promised myself a boat trip to Steamboat but it was 15 years later that I actually made the first of many trips to this area.

The famous west bank of Steamboat Slough has not changed much. The Delta's system of mooring, using willow branches and tree trunks, is still in use. The big changes are in the increased numbers of sleek cruisers always on the move up and down Steamboat along with the hundreds of smaller craft developed in the sixties for runabouting, water-skiing and beachheadings.

Steamboat Slough is another Delta waterway that has become the almost exclusive property of the pleasure boats. On Steamboat's east bank and levee, there is a fine, modern pleasure-boating complex, The Steamboaters. This area of the river is lined with deluxe floats. There is a fully equipped fuel service center and guest boats are welcome. A large area is lined off for the enjoyment and protection of beach swimmers. At the levee top, on the nearby country roadway, is The Steamboaters, a popular restaurant and cocktail lounge. From its huge windows, diners have a view of the yachts cruising the stretch where once the 200-foot steamboats battled for the passenger dollar.

Steamboat Slough provides a direct, 12-mile link between two sections of the Sacramento River. Using Steamboat cuts off a much longer, curving loop of the Sacramento down stream, past Walnut Grove and Isleton to Rio Vista.

In the early days of the big riverboats, the through trips and fastest schedules were routed over this slough that connected the two major segments of the Sacramento and cut off a number of miles, swift currents and the river towns of Walnut Grove and Isleton.

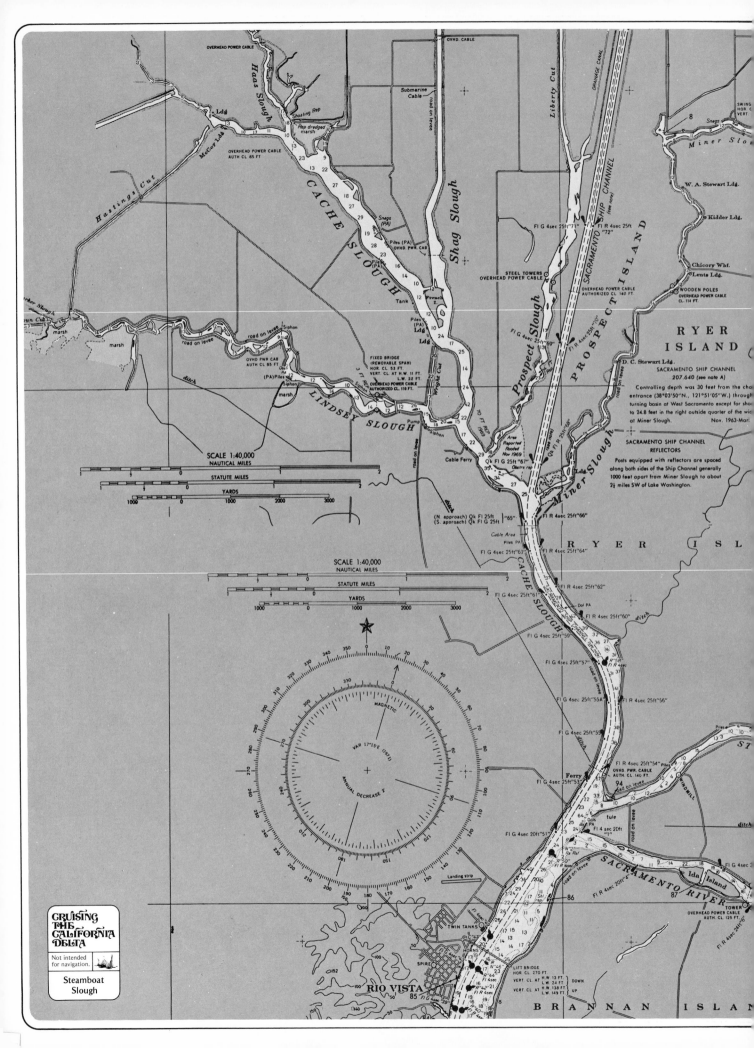

OVERHEAD POWER CABLE

Haas Slough

OVHD. CABLE

Submarine Cable

Ldg.

road on levee

Shoaling Rep

Rep dredged marsh

McCoy Lda.

Hastings Cut

OVERHEAD POWER CABLE
AUTH CL 85 FT

CACHE SLOUGH

Shag Slough

SWING
HOR
VERT

8

Snags

Miner Slou

W. A. Stewart Ldg.

FI G 4sec 25ft"71"

Liberty Cut

DRAINAGE CANAL

SACRAMENTO SHIP CHANNEL (see note)

FI R 4sec 25ft"72"

Kidder Ldg.

Snags
(PA)

Piles (PA)

OVHD. PWR. CAB.

Piles
(PA)

STEEL TOWERS
OVERHEAD POWER CABLE

OVERHEAD POWER CABLE
AUTHORIZED CL 140 FT.

Chicory Whf.

Lenta Ldg.

WOODEN POLES
OVERHEAD POWER CABLE
CL. 114 FT.

Parker Slough

Lindsey Slough

Montezuma Cut

marsh

marsh

road on levee

Siphon

ditch

OVHD PWR CAB
AUTH CL 85 FT

(PA)Piles

Siphon

Piles(PA)

Tank

French I.

Piles
(PA)

Ldg.

Ldg.

FIXED BRIDGE
(REMOVABLE SPAN)
HOR. CL. 53 FT.
VERT. CL. AT H.W. 11 FT.
L.W. 2? FT.
OVERHEAD POWER CABLE
AUTHORIZED CL. 118 FT.

Wright Cut

FI G 4sec 25ft"69"

Prospect Slough

FI R 4sec 25ft"70"

PROSPECT ISLAND

RYER
ISLAND

D. C. Stewart Ldg.

SACRAMENTO SHIP CHANNEL
207.640 (see note A)

Controlling depth was 30 feet from the cha
entrance (38°03'50"N., 121°51'05"W.) throug
turning basin at West Sacramento except for shos
to 24.8 feet in the right outside quarter of the wid
at Miner Slough.   Nov. 1963-Mar.

SACRAMENTO SHIP CHANNEL
REFLECTORS

Posts equipped with reflectors are spaced
along both sides of the Ship Channel generally
1000 feet apart from Miner Slough to about
2½ miles SW of Lake Washington.

Pump

LINDSEY SLOUGH

Siphon

road on levee

Miner Slough

Ldg.

Cable Ferry

Qk FI G 25ft"67"
Obstr rep

road on levee

Area
Reported
flooded
Nov 1969

SCALE 1:40,000
NAUTICAL MILES

STATUTE MILES

YARDS

(N approach) Qk FI 25ft
(S. approach) Qk FI G 25ft

"65"

FI R 4sec 25ft"66"

Cable Area
Piles PA

R Y E R   I S L

FI G 4sec 25ft"63"

FI R 4sec 25ft"64"

SCALE 1:40,000
NAUTICAL MILES

STATUTE MILES

YARDS

FI R 4sec 25ft"62"

ditch

FI R 4sec 25ft"60"

Dol PA

FI G 4sec 25ft"61"

FI G 4sec 25ft"59"

350   360   10
340   20
330   30
320   40
310
300   50
290   60
280
270   MAGNETIC   80
260
250   90
                                 100
240
230   VAR 17°15'E (1971)
220   110
210   120
200   ANNUAL DECREASE 3'
190   130
180   170   160   150   140

CACHE SLOUGH

FI G 4sec 25ft"57"

R"58"
FI R 4sec

FI G 4sec 25ft"55A"

FI R 4sec 25ft"56"

FI G 4sec 25ft"55"

Piles

FI R 4sec 25ft"54"

Piles

OVHD. PWR. CABLE
AUTH. CL. 140 FT.

94

Ferry

FI G 4sec 25ft"53"

road on levee

tule

WINDMILL

ditch

Dol
PA

FI G 4sec 20ft"51"

FI 4 sec 20ft"1"

Landing strip

SACRAMENTO RIVER

Ida
Island

FI R 4sec 20ft"4"

87

86

FI R 4sec 20ft"2"

TOWER

OVERHEAD POWER CABLE
AUTH. CL. 125 FT.

TWIN TANKS

FI R 4sec 2

HORNS

SPIRE

RIO VISTA

85

LIFT BRIDGE
HOR. CL. 270 FT.
VERT. CL. AT H.W. 13 FT.
L.W. 24 FT.   DOWN

VERT. CL. AT H.W. 138 FT.
L.W. 149 FT.   UP

FI G 4sec

BRANNAN   ISLA

*Steamboat Slough days. Top: Beach at the bend on down-river run.
Center, left to right: Sea Scout ship,* Captain Wrucke, *gets underway;
view of entry to Islands Marina atop Miner Slough. Bottom, left to right:
a sailboat hangs up on a mud bar; Spindrift YC boats at the marina.*

In the 1850s, the steamboat *New World* made a record run of five hours and thirty-five minutes between Sacramento and San Francisco, hours under the previous record. The fact she had killed a number of passengers when a steam line let go on Steamboat Slough didn't slow her down for the record run, either.

A few years later, the *Chrysopolis*, the 245-foot darling of all the rivermen, took Steamboat Slough out of Sacramento on New Year's Eve, 1861. With her 35-foot side-paddlewheels churning the slough slit at nearly 20 knots, *Chrysopolis* brought the time down to five hours and nineteen minutes, a record never equaled or surpassed by the other steamboats.

Among the first Sacramento River improvements made by the California state government to aid the steamboat traffic was the driving of a dolphin (bound together pilings) at the upper end of Steamboat Slough where the sandy beach on the point now attracts swimmers.

This dolphin aided the long, deep-draft boats, particularly the *Capital*, the longest of all at 277 feet and registering a surprising 2,000 gross tons. There was no way she could swing the channel turn on her own when coming down river. With the dolphin piles driven, the pilot could nose her bow into the cluster, drive the ship hard with the rudder over, and bring her around.

In his book, *Paddle-Wheel Days*, Jerry MacMullen, historian, and staff commodore of the San Diego Yacht Club, wrote this passage: "One day the *Antelope*, which had left Sacramento half an hour behind her, caught up with the *Sacramento* at the entrance to the narrow channel of Steamboat Slough. The *Antelope* tried to pass, but the *Sacramento* 'caught her suction' and forced her, crab-fashion, onto a mudbank, where she hung up. Captain Fouratt, who had her on that voyage, managed to get her off in a few minutes and started in hot pursuit; his passengers were very unhappy over the affair and began overhauling their six-shooters; but the captain assured them that he had an even better idea ... at Rio Vista he succeeded in jamming the *Antelope*'s bow into the *Sacramento*'s starboard quarter ... the other pilot rang up full astern but all the *Sacramento* succeeded in doing was to swing herself squarely across her rival's bow and was pushed sideways down the river for several miles before they decided to call it quits ...."

You won't find quite this kind of excitement on Steamboat Slough these days. But you will find warm seasons, fine deep water for boating, long runs for water-skiing and good beaches for swimming and picnics ashore. Steamboat takes you into Miner and Cache sloughs where there is good fishing and an occasional secluded, very quiet anchorage hidden among the tule stalks. At the top of Miner Slough is the excellent harbor of the new Island's Marina, the only covered moorage and visitors' harbor in that vicinity above Rio Vista's Delta Marina.

Famous old River Mansion has been restored to the elegance of its early years. There is a landing on the east side for visitors arriving by boat.

*An old river home is showing signs
of tumbling into one of the little
sloughs nearby Steamboat.*

One of Steamboat Slough's major tourist attractions is the River Mansion. This old, historic home is located less than two miles downstream from the bascule bridge at the head of the slough. Visiting yachtsmen may moor to the yacht landing on the east side.

River Mansion is one of the most elegant and stately old houses in all the Delta. The house is reminiscent of the great mansions built in the deep south before the Civil War, or some of the grand homes constructed in the late 1800s in San Francisco's posh Nob Hill district.

In the 1850s, Henry and Sophia Myers emigrated from Germany to the United States and made their way to California. Myers shunned the lure of gold and set to work developing a highly productive fruit ranch on 143 acres of Grand Island, fronting Steamboat Slough at this location. The riverboats loaded the fruit at a landing very near to where the pleasure boaters of today tie to the present visitors' float to tour the Mansion.

Louis William Myers, the son of Henry and Sophia, carried on the operations of the orchards and, in 1914, began to plan his future home. Construction was started in 1918. When it was completed, the four-storied house with 58 rooms had cost a half-million dollars, a huge sum in farming dollars in those days. Louis and his wife entertained lavishly. One winter, floods endangered the levees and Louis caught pneumonia while working in the thick of the emergency operations. He died but his wife stayed on at River Mansion with their eight children. Finally, the Myers family sold the property. Through the years, the property suffered from a succession of owners and inevitable neglect. Then the Millers bought River Mansion. Today, the visitor can stand on the grand staircase and revel in the restored beauty of the Grand Entry Hall and the Mansion's immense and lovely Ballroom. In the Colonnade Room, the Millers have installed the three-manual pipe organ from Sacramento's old Fox-Senator theater.

The halls are huge, and tastefully decorated with some very fine period paintings, etchings and valuable old maps and charts.

Some of the gorgeous rooms on the Mansion's main floor are also available for banquets. For special occasions, the first floor has been transformed into a deluxe restaurant and cocktail parlor. The Mansion is only available to the public for such purposes in certain seasons and arrangements should be made well in advance.

River Mansion's present owners are Mr. and Mrs. Richard A. Miller, California historians and authors.

The Millers have done a beautiful job of restoring and maintaining this old estate. They conduct tours of the mansion at very nominal rates, providing Delta tourists with one of the best bargains in the area.

The McCoy *of San Francisco moves along False River, skirting Franks Tract, on the St. Francis YC Tinsley cruise.*

12 The San Joaquin

The San Joaquin is the second largest navigable river in the Delta and pleasure-boat skippers find it the most useful in reaching a number of different cruising areas. The river branches out in paths. In parts of the lowlands, the San Joaquin twists itself into giant pretzel shapes as it meanders through the heart of the pleasure-boating section of the Delta.

This river has an easy way about it. Its numerous offshoots lead to fine anchorages and cruising reaches both to the north and south. It is banked with lush greenery and its many tule islands resemble rough-cut jewels.

Pleasant-sounding names promise pleasant surroundings. The San Joaquin is a name that sings and this river fulfills its promise. It begins at an altitude of 14,000 feet in the Sierra Nevadas, where the water trickles out of the rocks and melting snowfields.

Before it finally meets the Sacramento River to continue on a course through Suisun Bay and down to the great bay surrounding San Francisco, the San Joaquin is joined by eight major California rivers and 22 lesser streams. Its tremendous tidal flows help fill many of the popular sloughs within this great system of diked water we call the Delta.

More sloughs and rivers lead off the San Joaquin than from any of the other major channels. Beginning with the San Joaquin's own merging with the Sacramento, there are eighteen openings for entering and leaving: Dutch Slough to Bethel Island's main harbors and over to Old River by two different routes; False River to Fishermans Cut, along Franks Tract, then carrying back to the San Joaquin; Fishermans Cut off the river at Santa Clara shoal; Threemile Slough to the Sacramento; Sevenmile Slough that deadends; the Mokelumne River; Potato Slough; two reaches into Middle River; Little Connection Slough northward to the South Fork of the Mokelumne; Disappointment Slough; Whiskey Slough and Headreach Cutoff to Columbia Cut; Turner Cut south to the other Whiskey Slough and Empire Cut; Fourteenmile Slough, northward; Burns Cutoff around Rough and Ready Island; the Calaveras; the Smith Canal through residential Stockton; and the San Joaquin itself, where it leaves the deepwater channel at Stockton and meanders south toward the High Sierra.

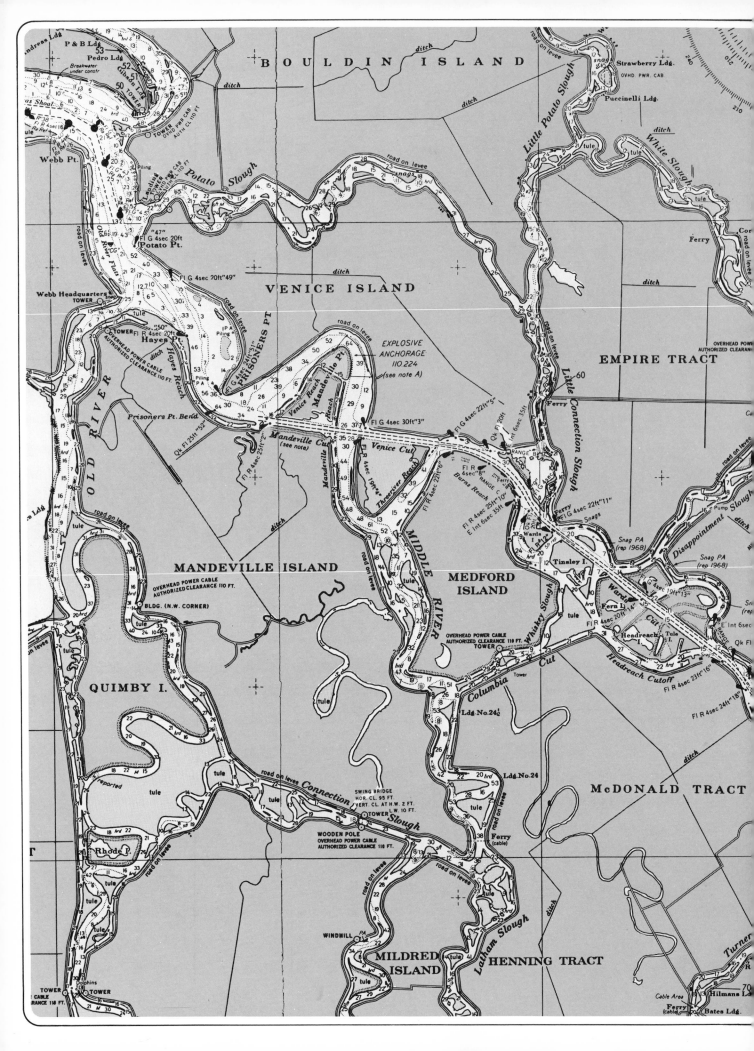

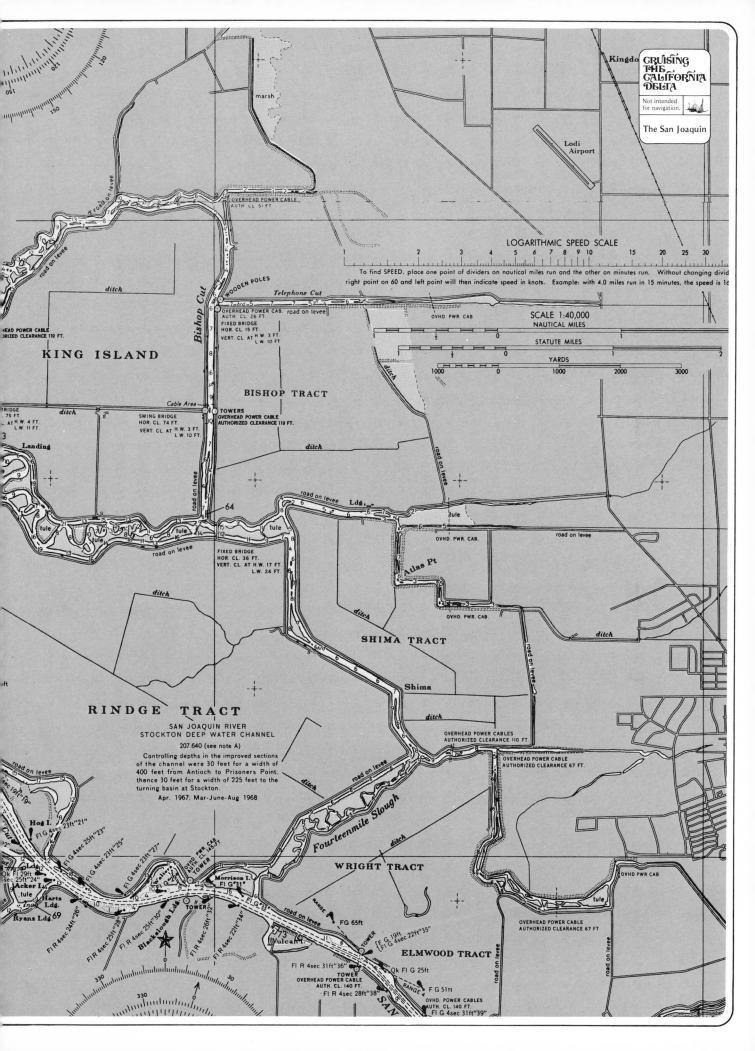

The San Joaquin, like the Sacramento River, was named twice and it was the second name that stuck. In 1772 Father Crespit, one of the early Spanish Catholic churchmen and explorers, sighted this river and named it San Francisco. Then, in 1805, while exploring its southern parts, Gabriel Moraga renamed it in honor of Saint Joachim. For a short period some pioneers and early historical accounts called it by one name and some by the other. By 1810, its second and present name was commonly accepted.

The San Joaquin River basin comprises nearly one-fifth of the entire state of California. This area measures approximately 300 by 130 miles. The basin is a rich, productive, enormous farmland, its irrigation provided by the Delta rivers and waterways. Since 1933 Stockton, 75 miles inland from the Golden Gate, has been an important deepwater San Joaquin river port contributing to the region's economic balance.

The main part of the San Joaquin from Antioch to Stockton is an easy, simple cruise. However, experienced Delta cruising people do not confine themselves to this route. They quickly learn that this is a river leading to many interesting places off the main river. They use the main river for short junkets turning off frequently to explore all its navigable reaches. A day of cruising on the San Joaquin usually involves leaving the main river and returning to it several times, only making one long continuous run when returning to your Delta home port in the evening.

There is always activity on the river and no crew is ever lonesome. To port, to starboard, another furrow is always being dug by a cruiser, sailboat or houseboat. The San Joaquin probably carries yachtsmen more passenger miles than any other river in the West.

This river has a number of wide reaches, several major shoals that must be run with careful attention to the navigational markers, and sections cut through by deepwater channels to carry deep-draft boats directly to Stockton. The result of modern dredging and channeling for commercial shipping, these cuts provide another facet of the personality of the San Joaquin. There are four major cuts, beginning at Prisoners Point—Mandeville, Venice, Wards and Hog. Each lies alongside an island of the same name. The cuts continue up the middle of the river to Stockton leaving the wide curving stretches of the river, with many island harbors and quiet estuaries, to the pleasure boats. The yachtsman is able to roam the waterways at ease among boats of his own size and kind while the big commercial vessels use the cuts. Most modern construction on the waterways takes away more than it adds to the pleasure of cruising but in the case of the San Joaquin the separate provisions made for the commercial vessel traffic has benefited the pleasure boaters and aided their enjoyment of the river.

A bend in the San Joaquin is a weekend haven for cruisers and sailboats.

They were stacked athwart (top, left) in October for the St. Francis YC Tinsley event. The St. Francis club's Delta landing (above) is at Tinsley Island.

Lost Isles harbor (above, left) and Windmill Cove (below, left) are favorite San Joaquin harbors. The ruins of old landings (above, right) stand where the Mokelumne empties into the San Joaquin. The river has its share of beaches, this one (below, right) with a beacon.

A distinctive private
landing on a little slough near the
Stockton Yacht Club.

Entering the San Joaquin for the first time, skippers soon realize that the river markers stand very high on pilings to favor pilots on the high bridges of towboats and freighters. Most markers are a combination of flasher lights and number boards. The numbers are in reflective paints and, on very bright days, are hard to read at a distance from the pleasure boats' lower level. Proceeding toward Stockton, the even numbers are to starboard and the odd numbers to port, a situation not always easily understood when one enters the river from a side channel. Shallow-draft cruisers and houseboats should adhere rather strictly to the channels, because it is easy to be hung up on the sandbars. Many a propeller has been damaged this way. Because the open river has an innocent look, one tends to become careless about aligning with the marked channels. However, if the skipper keeps to the channel, navigation is not difficult—at least not until a tule fog closes in.

Many navigational markers 20 feet and more above river level carry radar reflectors and, at difficult points and turns, are flanked with echo boards. If his boat is equipped with an air horn, the skipper can compute his distance from the markers by sounding the horn and counting the seconds it takes for an echo to return.

It was not quite so easy for early day river pilots. They conquered fog and darkness by bouncing steam whistle tones off of any shoreside barn or pile of drift that might return an echo. Charts for this area did not exist. Pilots recorded their new-gained knowledge of the shifting shoals by reading the current riffs and then passing the word to other captains. Keen and constant observation was required to avoid navigational hazards.

Cruising the area is enhanced by some knowledge of its history. It was a great event when Captain Warren piloted the *John A. Sutter* up the San Joaquin on the first scheduled steamboat run from San Francisco to Stockton, 120 years ago. It was also a banner day for the then little village when the *Sutter* arrived. Paddlewheels thrashed, visitors lined the ship's rails, the steam whistle pulled the boiler pressure down in blast after blast. Everyone who could get there was on hand when the *Sutter* was finally made fast to a big tree near Center Street. Stockton celebrated for several days.

Our own Delta cruising memories include our first trip on the San Joaquin in our own boat, headed for Stockton. We were in the middle of Mandeville Cut when we sighted a huge grain barge, moving in front of a snorting pusher tug, coming right at us. From our perspective, the barge appeared to shoulder the channel on each side. Its steel loading superstructure was weird and

our view across the sunlit waters was eerie. The multi-diesel drives were snorting and whining. There seemed to be no escape. We have encountered 20-knot passenger liners in narrow rocky straits but this experience had its own special terrors. Of course, abreast of the rig we found enough room to pass, but the tug's wake and the barge's bulk pushed out an undulating pattern that felt like a roller coaster beneath us for several miles. We have never encountered boat action like that since. It was one of boating life's unique experiences.

It is really the San Joaquin's surroundings that set it apart from other cruising rivers. The main channels are, for the most part, only fast routes to the more scenic areas, though they do attract many fishermen.

The lower river is sometimes open, sometimes cloistered. Its curving reaches toward the middle sweep tend to be more open, often windy and rather flat in color. Once inland, past the entrance to Potato Slough, the river and its byways take on more scenic color and a rather humid atmosphere.

Whenever one drops off the San Joaquin channel for a thousand yards or so, a great and interesting melange opens up for the boating family. There are public marinas, fine restaurants, fishing holes, private clubs, Delta-style harbors, protected estuaries, sites for rafting boats, fuel services, bait-box landings, and places for both swimming and water-skiing. There are places to go, a myriad of activities, and yet one feels remote from the realities of the clock and calendar, as if there were no city within hundreds of miles.

In this book, we treat the city of Stockton separately in Chapter 15 but no discussion of the boating on the San Joaquin River would be complete without at least a mention of Stockton's importance to the San Joaquin pleasure boater.

This great valley city of Stockton is a deep-sea port, a pleasure-boating port, a boatbuilding center and the home of many yacht and sailing clubs. In its strictest geographic sense, it belongs to the rich farmlands that surround it. Miles inland, it is the center of an enormous valley. Yet a great river moves right through its business and residential communities and it has a name in the pleasure-boating world that extends its reputation far beyond its size and importance as an inland city.

Stockton's waterfront is an extension of the river and includes a turning basin for ships. The San Joaquin River, coming out from the south through the lowlands, turns its back on the downtown city and wanders about through this course. The depths are generally good. It does not have great renown, but is a good small-boating and fishing stream. It has its separate links with Old River and Middle River and flows crookedly past the town of Tracy.

Cruising on the San Joaquin today, it is difficult to accept this rural stretch of the stream as having once supported a thriving steamboat and sternwheeler trade. The inland agricultural cities of Merced and Fresno were served by steamboats from the middle 1850s until close to the end of that century. This fact hardly seems possible to the highway traveler of 120 years later. The passenger boats also worked the tributarial Stanislaus and Tuolumne rivers. The narrow courses of these rivers hurried the development and use of sternwheelers in the Delta, because the wide sidewheelers were too wide for the course. In addition to eliminating the side paddle-wheels, sternwheelers were built with shallower draft hulls. This did away with the infamous "Chinese hold," a space up forward used, as its name implies, for packing in the hundreds of Chinese laborers for the trip upriver.

Early day captains and pilots were an independent breed, highly respected for their abilities to read a river. Those who worked the southern region in all kinds of visibility, day and night, were accomplished steersmen. The trying courses required great skill to prevent frequent and serious accidents.

The San Joaquin River is known to pleasure-boating people primarily for its flatland courses, where the levees of banked mud and the islands of heaped silt and tules play a major role in maintaining its bottomland fish populations. But romance and interest are added with the knowledge that the rural San Joaquin has its beginnings high on the southwest slope of Mount Goddard and is one of the many California mountain-born rivers that drain down through the foothills of the rugged Sierra Nevada to the valley below.

It is claimed that the San Joaquin is one of the few rivers in the United States that runs to the north, which it does before it turns for a long distance westward. Middle and Old rivers run north, too, but because they are smaller streams, they do not achieve a listing in that special category of USA rivers.

Our own cruising experiences on the San Joaquin have made us acutely aware of the infinite variety of activity that the river and its navigable offshoots offer the vacationing family crew.

Recently, we joined with friends who live and boat in the area year-round to get in some special San Joaquin River cruising aboard their resident boat. We started on a warm June morning—blue skies with cumulus clouds overhead. The river was light in color, a little drab at its wide spots away from the bank's shrubbery, but the scene was alive with boats moving in many directions. The rental houseboats were getting a good start on the weekend's hunt for places to go, their slow but steady paces playing tortoise to the faster hounds. There were several of the private houseboats that are becoming popular as cruisers on the Delta, including a large twin-hulled Carri-Craft that overtook us.

We had cut onto the river from near the Mokelumne and had not moved far before the skipper pointed toward the immense opening shown on the charts as Old River Flats. A river bar runs along it with a mean low water clearance of five feet. This big bulge was marked along the river's course by numerous pilings strung with yards and yards of wire netting. There is even a large gate between the two king piles. The gate, made of pipe and chicken wire, is padlocked and used for entry by official boats. The fence forms a great water pen where large numbers of striped bass have been transplanted. The striped bass has become one of California's finest food and game fish. A migrating sea bass, the popular striper is at home on the rivers and in the surf. This fish is also popular on the Atlantic Coast, and we have heard they were originally transplanted from a river in New Jersey to California waters.

The striped bass propagate well, but slowly. The California Fish and Game Department has continued stocking them. The Delta river pens keep out debris and intruders and create a good habitat for the young fish. These fine game fish are sought from boats, in the surf and from jetties and piers, and the topic of "the stripers" is a continual one in Delta fishing circles.

This particular San Joaquin cruising day moved along pleasantly fast. Without going more than a dozen miles along the river's main course, we turned off into at least ten interesting smaller channels, explored the harbors of several private clubs, put into the harbors of three riverside eating places, and visited a score of attractive anchorages where fine-looking boats were drawn up to their anchors and tree-lines. We were back off the river by dark. In succeeding days in the area, we rounded out previous cruises by just fanning out over all of the long waterways that tie in to the San Joaquin. There are innumerable possibilities for boating on this river and, with a little pleasant lagging in favorite harbors, a very memorable summer could be spent this way on the San Joaquin.

One of our most memorable Delta cruises involving the San Joaquin River area started at the St. Francis Yacht Club in the shadow of the Golden Gate Bridge.

Those who moor their boats in the dozens of marinas around San Francisco Bay are unusually privileged yachtsmen. They enjoy the flexibility of racing, cruising and sailing on challenging waters. On the Bay, they have exceptional views of city towers and hillside homes. Then they can tune out the city skyline and be out to sea in a matter of minutes, with the Pacific's blue under their bows.

Yet they are also uniquely privileged because they can drop all of this astern and be afloat in the entirely different world of the Delta within a couple of hours. That they appreciate and seek these contrasts in their pleasure boating is demonstrated by the fact the St. Francis Yacht Club's snuggery is located among the narrow channels and tall tules of the Delta at Tinsley Island.

This cruise, our most recent on the Delta, began at the end of September. At Tinsley, the St. Francis Yacht Club was holding its fourteenth annual invitational gathering of yachtsmen from many California ports and from the Pacific Northwest. Dignitaries from the East Coast, Hawaii, England, France and Australia were also present, for the event.

Tinsley Island is a superb vacational yachting club site, abutting the San Joaquin at a point between Little Connection and Disappointment sloughs, two-thirds of the way from Antioch to Stockton.

All relaxed cruising is good; on some beautiful days, with the right blend of river water, sky and clouds, it can become great. As one old-timer once said to me, "When you catch a real good day on the river, tie down on it like a sawlog and tow it with you."

This day was deliciously cool and sparkling when, around 0830 hours, we began dropping the St. Francis Yacht Club's home clubhouse and the Golden Gate Bridge far behind the transom traveler. This was a day of which the San Francisco skippers had a right to brag, but did not need to. The rest of us bragged for them.

We set off for Tinsley Island, and I was pleased to be approaching it from "down bay" for a change. The cruise proved unmistakably that every different approach to a beautiful river turns the cruise into a new experience. This time, eight of us were aboard Gene Trepte's Stephens-designed sloop *Brushfire*, from San Diego. Some of us, on the return trip three days later, would be with George Sturges, aboard his heavy cruiser from Newport Harbor.

Sailboats leave a quiet channel for the San Joaquin. The river is hidden behind the long tule island.

We lounged on the cockpit pads and moved around *Brushfire*'s decks. There were few duties and no watches except for the individual crew members watching everything in sight in the blending sea and landscapes studded with boats.

It was a treat to have along St. Francis' Tim Moseley, the renowned skipper of the *Orient*, a Bay Area and San Joaquin veteran yachtsman, who spiced the seven-hour run with his humorous homilies and many interesting items concerning the backgrounds of the landmarks along the way.

The change from the coast's influence was evident as we passed the last of the nostalgic Bay lighthouses, out of service on its jutting rock, well-painted by perching seabirds. Out ahead was the first of the tidal rips, where fresh water and silt get shouldered around by sea water and salt in a natural standoff.

Another hour or so and we were in the narrows where Chipps Island juts into the down sweep of the Sacramento River. This island, almost a peninsula, defines the westernmost end of the Delta. The pilots have to know its characteristics day and night, in light, dark and fog, because the few miles around and above Chipps are critical in finding either the Sacramento or the San Joaquin.

We changed course to the east, watching Pittsburg's yacht harbors drop away, and made way down New York Slough for Antioch and the beautiful San Joaquin. This is the shortest and, to me, the most appealing course.

New York Slough's name is a carryover from the era of passenger schedules on the Sacramento. At the start of these riverboat runs, this tiny port was pompously named "New York of the Pacific" in the hope it would grow to become a metropolis to match its namesake. Coal to fuel the steam-driven commerce of the rivers was found near Mount Diablo. It was low-grade coal, but nonetheless welcome, and was brought down to a landing named Black Diamond, near the "New York" site. As the dreams of a second New York City faded, the site was renamed "Pittsburg," echoing the Pennsylvania city and its nearby coalfields. But "New York" remained the name of the waterway or slough in front of Pittsburg.

On this particular cruise we formed as exciting a commodore's line of California "fighting ships" as ever headed up the San Joaquin. The pleasure-boat fleet was enormous, strung out in voluntary formation as it throbbed past the aged Antioch riverfront, the huge bridge west of Antioch, and the modern marinas in their protected slots. In the fleet were many of the winners in local and long-distance racing, honored for their one-thousand-mile and two-thousand-mile escort duty runs during the transocean races. Alongside were several 30- to 40-foot one-design yachts. All were deep at the waterline, carrying among them a total of 680 passengers to the Tinsley weekend. Many commodores and staff commodores, international race committeemen, naval architects and America's Cup crewmen and club-emblem wearers were present as crew or guests.

It is on autumn days such as this, just one day away from October, that the western yachtsman should count his blessings, reflecting that his eastern and midwestern comrade is putting his craft under wraps for the winter. Yet, here we were, moving past Dutch Slough's entry to Bethel Island on a windless late September morning, with temperatures rising into the seventies and everyone changing into summer deck clothing.

On this trip, we had a good look at Big Break and Franks Tract, examples of lowland acreage ruined when the soft peat and mud levees failed to hold against the winter floods of earlier years.

We were on the open San Joaquin for another four miles, and then swung sharply to starboard into False River. The scenery is typically Delta on the four miles past Taylor Slough, past Fishermans Cut to the point where Franks Tract, the immense lake that was once a great farm, lies dead ahead.

Then we swung along Washington Cut, with the tule islands in the center and thin lines of broken levees barely holding a channel for us. On this day, fishermen had a polyglot group of big cruisers and small boats on Franks Tract and we could see them over the berms and through the tules.

We next moved up Old River to the San Joaquin and the attractive final leg of the trip into Tinsley.

We saw a great deal on this cruise: a couple of low islands which will be in trouble unless the digger-dredges pile on some more peat; the many little landings to the duck blinds, a reminder that this is one of the great wild bird flyways; and places near Tinsley which are famous for frog hunting, a reminder that the World's Frog Jumping Championships are held in the San Joaquin Valley every year.

At the cruise's end, back in the Spanish-style St. Francis Yacht Club, several of us talked of the infinite variety of scenery and sport available to the Northern California pleasure-boat skippers. They have both the California Delta and the San Francisco Bay for their playground. They are lucky sailors indeed.

You can fish the open river, too, and many do just that on the San Joaquin.

The Potato Sloughs

Big and Little

Potato and Little Potato sloughs are major routes in the system of waterways related to the San Joaquin and the Mokelumne rivers. Though neither is very impressive as a cruising venture, they are handy connectors for the skipper seeking a harbor to absorb the hook quickly or hold a springline from the brushy shoreline. Most Delta skippers visit them often, even if only to breeze across them enroute to other boating destinations.

When first cruising the Delta in our own boat, we visited the triangle where three big waterways meet at Terminous. Later, in a conversation with a Power Squadron skipper from Southern California who was a veteran of Delta cruising, I tried to relate the area to my charts and spoke of "Potato Slough" as though there were only one This river rat gleefully challenged me with the simple question, "Big Potato? Or Little Potato?" His terminology has stuck with us. It sets the two apart in a

A former ferry landing at the Little Potato junction to the Delta's Staten Island.

13

92

positive, memorable way, as do the simple rhymes such as "Red sky at night—sailor's delight . . ."

The Potatos are excellent sloughs for cruising from one area to another. Their interesting berms and islands are replete with places to hide and places to speed. The surrounding countryside adds to their beauty.

Terminous, which is being revived as a marina and houseboat rental center, was once an important shipping port in river freighting. At one time it was also the terminal for a little ferry that chugged over to the roadway on Staten Island. This was the Delta's own Staten Island ferry.

Little Potato Slough's short route is filled with interesting scenery and many winding turns. Its flow is swift at Terminous, drawing a tremendous amount of water off the Mokelumne's South Fork, dropping it down past White Slough and into Little Connection. Near Terminous, Little Potato Slough produces some typical river scenery with many bridges, little islands and tree-lined banks. Little Potato makes a convenient junction with the parent Potato Slough.

Below White Slough, Little Potato widens and serves up some great islands and river shelters. The beautiful private harbor estuary of Grindstone Joe's Association lies off this section. Power Squadron's Devil's Isle club is at White Slough.

The Potato Sloughs were probably named for the potato crops produced in the region years ago. Venice Island, a fine piece of farmland bordering on Potato Slough, has a Potato Point.

Big Potato has two outstanding attractions for the cruising family. It brings together many cruising alternatives by connecting the several forks of the Mokelumne with the San Joaquin in its spacious secondary, east-and-west running passage. In addition, it supplies some of the best anchorages in the Delta.

Potato Slough runs parallel to the Mokelumne's South Fork which lies just to the north. It leaves the San Joaquin in the west and is linked back into the San Joaquin by way of Little Connection Slough. The western half of Potato has several large tule islands and some very wide turns. Its runs are easy. There is a choice of courses on either side. The tule islands separate the courses most of the way, so each side is like a wholly separate slough.We advise skippers to stay to one bank of the levee or the other on a single run. The terrain can be confusing when roaming Big Potato.

At top: At Terminous on Little Potato, former river freight sheds are converted to marinas. Bottom: A favorite anchorage on Big Potato in a tule crescent.

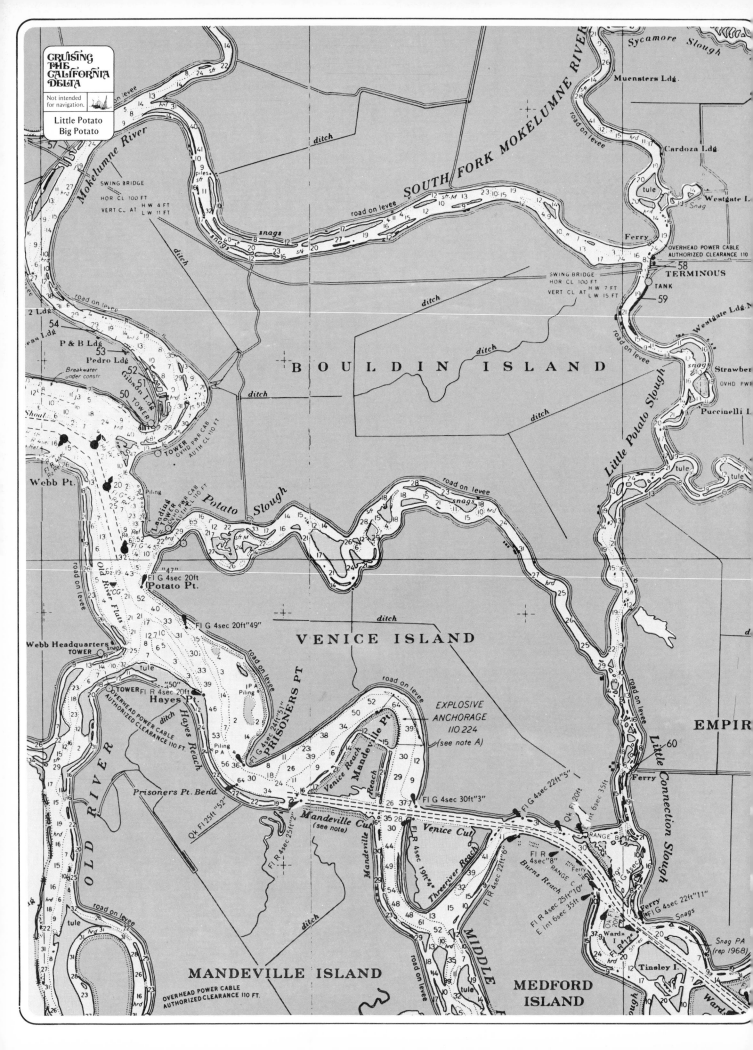

Big Potato's outstanding anchorages are set apart by its massive tule islands, its wide slough bed and the snaking waterways created by these islands. Two of these coves are especially popular. One is within a cluster of three islands. The other is formed by the combination of six berms, overgrown with reeds and willows. At these island points, the slough is at least a thousand yards wide. Boats at anchor are protected from passing wakes. The strong breezes of the open water are knocked down to a whisper most of the time. The area is popular with swimmers and vacationers who want a quiet anchorage for a long visit.

In its way, Big Potato is just as popular as The Meadows and much closer to the marinas of the Mokelumne and the San Joaquin areas.

Big Potato can be filled with action one hour—quiet and relaxing the next. It is a heavily wooded retreat. The beauty of good family boating is evident here with children splashing about on everything that floats, a camaraderie running between the cockpits and the good smells of dinners cooking among the tules. Our impressions are that charcoal artists of the afterdeck brazier are at their best in this setting.

Trees and water meet and merge in typical Delta slough landscaping.

Activity on the Potato Sloughs and a wide variety of boats and scenery. The two Potatos are excellent sloughs for cruising, replete with berms and islands providing places to hide and places to speed.

We got our first introduction to the mooring style of the Delta on our first cruise of Potato Slough. I made a slip-line system for holding our bow to one of the harbor's willow limbs. The tide was in but we had a hard time reaching strong limbs. Finally secured, we set out the stern anchor. Our overnight stay was pleasant and uneventful. But in the morning, when the tide was down, the line up in the tule cleats was out of reach and the slip-system was hung up. There was a big stretch of Delta goo between our bow and that little tree, so we cut loose at our bow cleat and donated a fine hunk of new nylon mooring line to the birds.

Big Potato and its shelters are bright and warm during the summer days and cruising families will enjoy the area's waters and recreational possibilities.

Top: A cable ferry down Little Connection. Big Potato is linked back into the San Joaquin by way of Little Connection Slough. Bottom: Well-known Herman's and Helen's, just south of the junction of Big and Little Potato Sloughs.

97

The Waters of
Old and Middle Rivers

When you look at the many courses, channels within channels, and the angles of sloughs and cutoffs in the Delta's "south forty" during daylight you cannot help wondering about the impossibility of navigating them on foggy nights. Tule fogs come often here and nights can be very dark. It is not surprising that we do not hear more about regular steamboat schedules in the Old River and Middle River country. Tracking a compass needle over courses from one side to the other of some of these streams must have presented river pilots with serious problems. There are many former farm landings and commercial vessels did use these rivers. But the very obstacles that must have been encountered by the steamboats help turn these waters into a great area for pleasure boating.

South of the San Joaquin, Turner Cut provides some lovely scenery.

14

South of the San Joaquin, the waters of Old and Middle rivers spread out in many different patterns. The weather is a little warmer. Crews notice these changes beginning to take place soon after the green corridor of the San Joaquin is dropped behind.

Many skippers overlook these intriguing channels. They get into the habit of cruising the northern Delta waters and do not find the time to explore these southern rivers. But here are a couple of good daytime cruises in new surroundings that can add new spice to your Delta galley stew.

Fishermen value these southern rivers and they have worked them for years from every size of smaller craft. The miles of slow-flowing waters of Old and Middle rivers create fine fishing holes and banked-up reaches. There are many small landings, boat rentals, and bait shops catering to pleasure boaters and fishermen.

This is also the land of the speed breed, the people who have become adept at fast boating, at riding the water slats for long sunny hours of their brand of fun. The charts show better than words the miles of open water and the long straight courses that are available for water-skiing.

But the lovers of fast sports do not seem to bother the crews who prefer leisurely cruising. There are crooked reaches, straight cuts, and sizable tule islands setting off the quiet niches. There are many fine coves which provide pleasant anchorages. Most of the larger yachts bring in smaller boats to use for their hours of faster boating sports.

This interesting complex of rivers extends south to Tracy and Byron and west to a vertical line running even with Bethel Island.

There are really three rivers: Old River, Middle River and the section of the San Joaquin as it passes Modesto and enters the deep, wide channels that work west from Stockton. This segment of the San Joaquin is much like Old and Middle rivers in appearance, not like the main river scenery and flow.

These two streams (Old and Middle rivers) are classical in the way they wander around low land masses. Old River picks up from the southern San Joaquin and slithers 12 miles westward, creating gnarly Tom Paine Slough and a half-dozen other cuts and connections. Then Old River moves on to the north for another 20 miles, tying into the San Joaquin near Bethel Island. Along the way its channels create many opportunities for interesting side trips. If all of these courses were straightened out and "laid end-to-end" they would make a ribbon of water approximately a hundred miles long.

Middle River has the same characteristics. It opens in the south off Old River and empties into the San Joaquin by two short forks which are separated by the big Venice tule bed island.

Ferries are the connecting links between Delta island highways. The newer breed makes use of diesel instead of cable. Cars are carried free and schedules are when you're ready. Top: Diesel ferry near Tiki Lagun. Bottom: Cable ferry facility on Middle River.

The entrance to
Indian Slough is marked by a souvenir
from a long ago flood.

Years of digging for levee building materials has deepened their channels and left many canallike cuts. Very few of these are called sloughs—most are called cuts or canals. In creating them, fine waterways for cruising were developed.

Most cruising visitors do not comprehend the century-long endeavor that has gone into reclaiming and protecting this land, much of which lies below river level.

Clamshell-type dredges have been used for years. But methods and tools were crude in the early days and the Chinese coolies provided the mainstay of backbreaking labor.

Even though there is heavy machinery to move the peat and silt now, another problem persists. Soil for the top must not be dug at the expense of undermining the footing. Marshy soil is unstable.

Some of the reaches are crammed with large tule islands and there are many channels weaving around them. This condition was created when the wide, shallow beds of the two rivers were deepened by the steady bite of big steel dredging claws swinging from one side of a barge to the other. Because the length of the dredging booms limited their reaching circle, this method of construction created a special pattern for cruising. In its broader aspects, the determination of earlier residents to create rich, stable farming lands provided today's yachtsmen and fishermen with deeper channels and more retreats.

Roberts Island is typical. It was one of the successful early reclamation projects. Today, it is a great agricultural producer, etched by the San Joaquin, Turner Cut, Whiskey Slough and Middle River.

While it is difficult to be entirely sure, it is believed that the first levee was built around Grand Island by an early-day farmer, Reuben Kerchevel, in about 1850. His levee was designed to shut out the high waters of the Sacramento and what is now called Steamboat Slough.

By the 1870s, land reclamation was being undertaken in a serious way. In *Fortune Built by Gun*, Richard A. (Bob) Miller, owner of the historic Mansion Building on Steamboat Slough, tells the story of Joel Parker Whitney, an early Delta pioneer. One chapter deals with the reclamation of Roberts Island. About 1872, Whitney became interested in the overflow lands and found that most had been taken up. He wrote of making an excursion with land groups, members of various land firms and some "gentlemen from Ohio and Kentucky." Aboard the paddlewheel steamer *Flora*, they visited Roberts, Sherman, Grand and Union islands.

The account is a long and involved history of the way Whitney made his judgments of land values, present and future, and then worked out his bids and shrewd proposals. Whitney finally obtained a number of acres on Roberts Island. A reclamation company was capitalized for $850,000, a considerable sum of money for those days. Whitney wrote a promotional booklet describing these freshwater tidelands to encourage others to invest in Delta land developments.

The Chinese labor used in the Delta reclamation projects was available in gangs through Chinese contractors at about fifteen cents per cubic yard of dirt moved. The gangs ranged in size from several hundred to a thousand men. Cruising along the levees they built, one can visualize the hum of activity created by the human force of these men working everywhere with their shovels and peat cutters. Their tools were primitive. This was cheap, human labor, totally unskilled and, although the Chinese were hard workers, there were obvious drawbacks and progress was slow.

Parkey Whitney was a brilliant man, a far-seeing planner. He observed the primitive methods and rate of productivity. He reasoned that this labor was actually not cheap at all. Whitney knew that mechanization was imperative. So he designed and had a Stockton shipbuilder construct two steam-driven earthmovers, mounted on boat hulls, carrying 50-foot booms. These devices lift about three cubic yards per bucket. His costs were reduced immediately to around five cents per cubic yard of earth moved. At the same time, his machines made accessible more of the river soil. Thus, Whitney put the first successful mechanical dredges into operation in the Delta, building better levees and doing the job faster at lower cost.

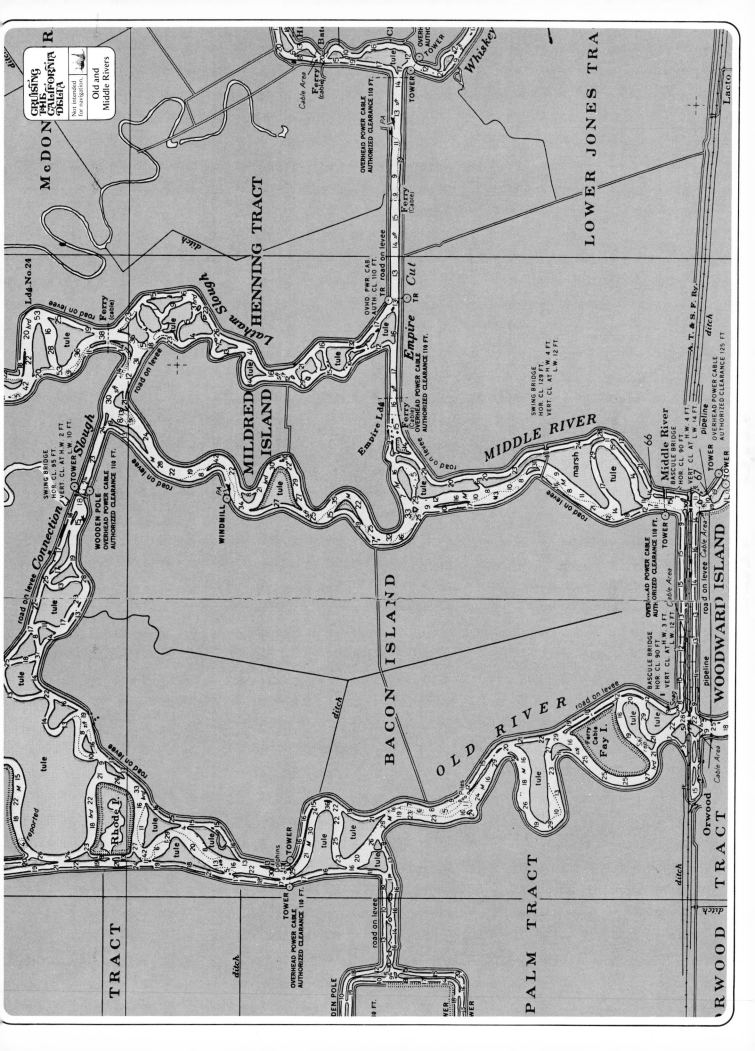

At the same time, Whitney saw the need to create large companies to finance the full reclamation of these valuable lands. In organizing such enterprising groups, Whitney set a pattern in financing these types of projects. Bob Miller, who researched his subject well and possesses the Whitney papers and records, gives Whitney's concepts credit for the eventual structure of California's agricultural "organization" and feels Whitney's dynamic impetus was instrumental in converting California's vast Delta swamplands into arable and highly productive agricultural property.

The name "Old River" is given to the complex of all of the individual waterways which branch crookedly over much of the Delta land to the south. The open waterways here are grand and timeless in their cloaks of dikeland shrubbery. Other stretches, spotted with old

bridges and abandoned ranch buildings, have an early-century feeling. The two are in marvelous balance for pleasing cruisers' tastes.

At the start of a cruise on Old River, one perceives the differences in air and scenery in this area south of the San Joaquin. This lower sector of the Delta contains at least 500 miles of separate turning, twisting channel courses, lacing an area that is only about 30 miles across in each direction. As is the case in other parts of the Delta, descriptive names have not been established for this distinct inner region. We are in the habit of referring to it as "South of the San Joaquin." This identifies the region very well, taking into account everything from Stockton to Bethel Island and as far south from the river as any one cares to cruise, fish and enjoy recreation on the water.

From this perspective, the mast vies successfully with the familiar line of Delta poplars. Old and Middle River courses are popular with the sailboat crowd.

Stout Curlew *(at top) starts her day's cruise. A rendezvous (center) at Columbia Cut near Middle River. Tiki Lagun (bottom) is an extremely popular marina mooring on Turner Cut.*

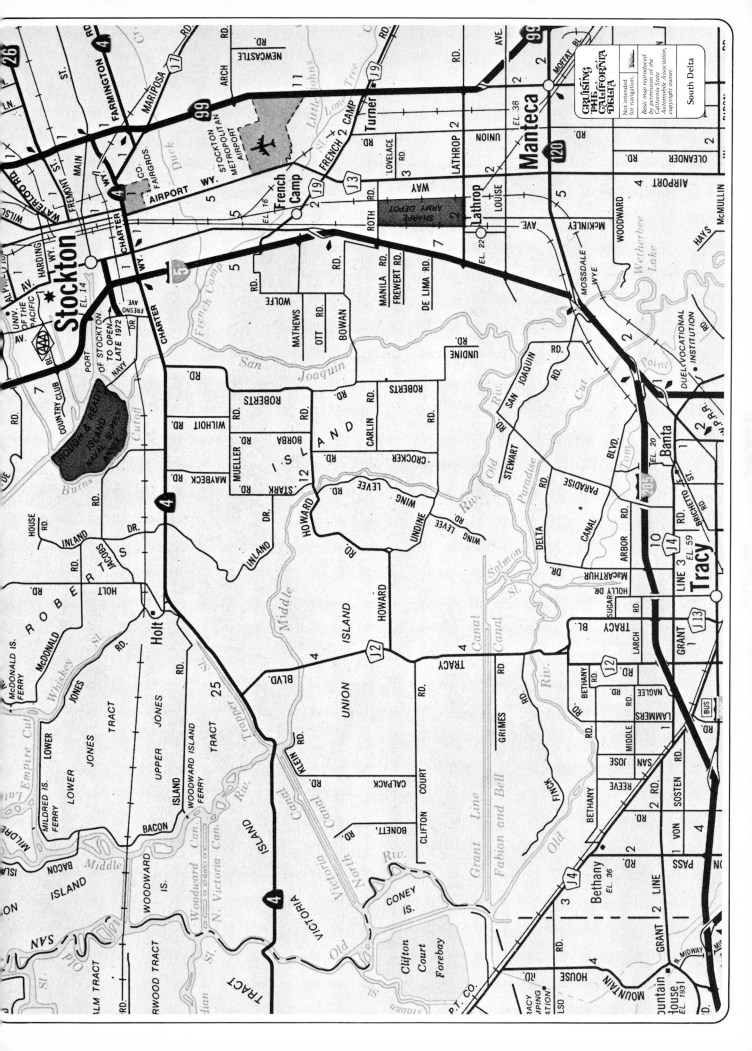

As a cruising family we feel that all good small-boat cruising comes down to setting a personal plan for the crew's outing. Planning is particularly necessary in the southern region of the California Delta where there are dozens of courses and no one can cover them all in anything short of a month. During the summer of 1971, from early July to the end of September, we cruised the Delta. On certain days each week we would visit and revisit "down south" of the San Joaquin in the Old and Middle rivers' area including some fine cruises on the main river course itself.

In company with many Delta yachtsmen, we prefer the smaller cruising boat in this region where there are many waterways to explore and frequent changes of course. In the smaller cruising boat, the skipper can idle, drift, backtrack, or lay down a long-ribboned wake when he gets the urge for speed. It is easier to get off the

The area south of the San Joaquin is a playground for those who love the water. There are many river beaches and a lot of fine stretches for water skiing.

anchor and prowl, pursuing oddments lying off the main track.

Our own cruising south of the San Joaquin has been done in a small cruiser operating on a cruising plan that permitted us to enjoy as much of the variety of scenery and activity in this area of the Delta as possible.

On the most recent of these cruises, we started by working our way along the San Joaquin for a few miles before we turned into the harbor of the Lost Isles Club, a marina open to the boating public. They have a restaurant and outdoor area that is extremely attractive. The spacious floats are well-protected and can handle large groups of pleasure craft. Clubs on group cruises frequently stop here. This marvelous little boating byway is a cut in Acker Island (a place seldom referred to by name) and it fronts on Twentyonemile Cut, a 1,300-yard-long appendage of the San Joaquin.

Discovery Bay developers direct buyers coming by boat. A steamboat replica takes customers to home sites.

Historical remnants: Abandoned structures; warning piling marking old wrecks; pampas grass planted to hold levee earth.

Our cruising plan then took us back to Threeriver Reach. This is a section of the big horseshoe in the San Joaquin where Middle River enters the main stream. Its depths run a surprising 30 to 60 feet. There are many boating courses and the tule islands are big and varied until Middle River settles into a big open-boot shape. Columbia Cut shows up here and one can angle back through it to Whiskey Slough and Tinsley Island, the latter area very popular with frog hunters. Alternately, one can work back up the San Joaquin for a few miles to Lost Isles and Turner Cut. Turner Cut harbors Tiki Lagun, a very fine marina and restaurant. There is no end to the choice of routes through this area of the Delta.

Columbia Cut itself is favored with several long reaches, interesting large tule islands and ample room for large and small boats to tie up to the brush shoreline. This course is, in general, a very attractive and useful site for all boating pleasures. It also has the advantage of being close to the main stream.

From Columbia Cut, we moved on to the next big-boot shape on Middle River, less than a mile below. There are two big islands here, near a landing known as No. 24, a designation that has survived from riverboating days. These two islands force the river outward into a half-mile-wide stream, creating fine estuaries for boating and anchoring away from the busier channels.

On the south side of the first island are the big quadrangles known as Five Fingers (see Chapter 16) but none of these notches appear on the charts. On a warm day this stretch is open to the sky. The banks are brushy; the river sparkles with blue water in contrast to the green colors so typical of many other Delta courses.

Boats are on the move here and water skiers are numerous, but the waterfowl stay near the grasses, paying little attention to the activity. All through this area, fish and other wildlife are abundant. In the fall, great migrations of wild fowl are on the wing, feeding on the farms and in the marsh grasses. Fall is duck hunting time in the Delta and many visiting hunters return to this area every year.

There is a cable ferry between McDonald Tract and Mandeville Island, one of the many connecting the Delta island roads with one another. Many of the newer ferries, designed for short crossings, have abandoned the cables and now use diesel power with conventional propellers. These ferries add a picturesque quality to the boating scene in the Delta in addition to being vital links in commercial and passenger movement through the area.

Near the ferry crossing, between McDonald Tract and Mandeville Island, Middle River runs into Latham Slough where the tule islands are big and the courses are varied. The river makes a sharp turn along a cut and continues south. At this point, a chart is the easiest way to understand the complex. Empire Cut has two ferries and reaches back over to Whiskey Slough. Middle River goes down to where Woodward Canal connects it with Old River. The whole pattern repeats itself in the different winding streams, dredged cuts, harbors and open stretches—more variety and complexity than there is anywhere else. The Delta navigational charts are a must for this area and will aid in planning the daily cruises and explorations.

We ended our own cruise by returning by way of Old River. Along our homeward bound route were great stands of pampas grass stretching out in clusters a hundred yards wide. The grass was in feathery full bloom, standing high against the blue sky, out like a pennant in a five-knot breeze. The pampas grass and tules are examples of the interesting natural growth in these open sections. Deep in the high trees and lush greenery up against the banks, excellent harbors can be made in the covered mooring ports of many abandoned industrial operations. There is enough of interest here to hold the attention of a cruising visitor for hours on end.

The old bridges are excellent scenic backdrops for the photography buffs. Old riverboat hulks are sometimes sighted, half submerged, alongside pilings. The only signs of the old commercial landings are the tightly driven rows of piling, most of which are now rotted off at river level. Many of the homes command marvelous views of river reaches and the steady movement of pleasure boats on the water.

In common with other attractive areas in California's interior, interesting changes are being made in Delta living and the success of these projects will influence future developments. Unlike harbor areas in population centers along the coast, the Delta's southern region has had little or no housing, club and estate developments on specially dredged streams or man-made lakes. Now, however, the huge Delta Discovery Bay development started in 1971 is placing homes, roadways and a yacht harbor complex 2 miles east of Byron on Highway No. 4 and directly off the waters of Indian Cut. Indian, which has several variations in name on the charts, is a fine, partly cloistered waterway flowing off Old River near Woodward and North Victoria canals. Boats in Discovery Bay will be able to fan out through the whole Delta, though some sectors of the development will feature enclosed lakes.

*The Delta bridges. A scenic delight—
often a boating hazard. Below are
two we photographed on Old River.*

*On a Middle River cruise, below, a dog
shares a rubber float ride and we spotted a
comfortable landing set up for fishing.*

On a reverse plan, garages will face the streets and picture windows will look out on the family's private boat landing. There will be a whole new way of life on Old River.

On our last Delta cruise south of the San Joaquin, we moved northward up Old River, homeward bound in the late September afternoon sun. We selected the Holland Cut side of the river. This course, a 20-foot-deep creation of the diking dredge, runs for four amazing straight miles. Speedboating and water-skiing are at their best here.

We passed Old River's wide loop at Mandeville Island, near where the old riverboat, *The Navajo*, now stands reproachfully high and dry in the middle of the farm fields. We moved out across the eastern face of Franks Tract. Here, the collapsed levees of a once great farm now barely delineate the shoreline of Old River. During two years of great floods that finally destroyed the levees and farmland, bundles of tule grass were tied together and dropped in behind crudely driven piling in a vain, dirty and wet attempt to save the fertile fields. Knowing that the waters flow over old buildings, pilings and machinery, we are always a little sad when crossing

Franks Tract. If care is taken, there is no danger but the prevailing afternoon breezes funnel across the open tract keeping the water bumpy. Skippers should stay alert.

Leaving Franks Tract, we were soon abreast of the channel that cuts into the San Joaquin. We had passed the sunken remains of old Irish and Fletcher landings. The 110-foot towers carrying overhead power cable frame the Old River entrance and are useful landmarks. Similar towers throughout the region, and clearly shown on the charts, are reliable sight beacons helping to reckon position from a low-profile boat when trees on the dikes obscure vision.

It is a truism that every cruise around the Delta ends where it begins. On this particular occasion, we had a grand twilight homeward run, a quick turn into Potato Slough to look around, a fine cruise up the Mokelumne back to our starting point. No matter where you are, a friendly home port, even a borrowed one, is the perfect ending to a day afloat.

Delta yachtsmen need to allow plenty of time for their cruising explorations of the southern region of the Delta—a most rewarding area. A month of leisurely cruising days just might be sufficient time to log it.

Stockton

Deep Water Port

Stockton is an unusual yachting city. Large and small pleasure craft can cruise up the San Joaquin, move in to the eastern end of the deepwater channel, and moor at the foot of the downtown area. Crews can walk from this point into the center of the city.

Stockton is also a seaport. It serves the commerce of one of the world's great agricultural valleys. With a population of more than 107,000, it is second only to Sacramento in size and importance among the Delta's cities. It is remarkable that a 35-foot water depth—deep enough for ocean cargo boats—extends so far into California's dry interior. It is a credit to the men who were determined to improve its status as a port, a position that was established back in 1849 when the *John A. Sutter* steamed up to the foot of Center Street and secured its mooring lines to a big tree in the town that Charles W. Weber founded. For a time it was called "Tuleberg," a name that would hardly fit Stockton today.

For those who enjoy days ashore, Stockton is heartily recommended. It is a good place to shop in city stores or to obtain marine supplies. It is a major boatbuilding and repair center. It has launching sites, guest moorages, and all the necessary marine services and accommodations. The downtown area's old buildings are being rebuilt.

Stockton's deep water channel terminates at its downtown city center. The Uptown Yacht Harbor's marina is located there. The concrete embarcadero is new.

15

In peacetime and wartime, Stockton has always been a boatbuilding town. For more than a half-century, the yachting community has respected the well-known Stephens' yachts built in Stockton by a family of designers and builders of quality cruisers and sailboats.

Ladd's Stockton Marina fostered the first rental pontoon houseboat fleets. This large marina now attracts boating visitors from all over the world.

The Stockton Yacht Club on the Calaveras River is in the most enjoyable of settings. Its grounds, studded with great poplars, slope down from the clubhouse to the landings in elegant style.

The Stockton Sailing Club is active all year developing local sailing programs. Their activities give a strong affirmative answer to the common question, "Is there good sailing on the Delta?" Stockton Sailing Club members are always ready to talk up the joys of sailing on the San Joaquin River.

Calcagno's Marina, in the heart of the city, conducts Delta excursion trips with an excellent new passenger boat, designed for the best viewing of the local rivers with maximum comfort for the traveler. It is the only such project now offering this service and will bring tourists to the greenery of the Delta waterways.

Stockton's old waterfront is being rebuilt. In part of the area a new complex of Chinese shops and restaurants puts its street signs (below, left) in Chinese characters. Another view (below, right) of the city's waterfront redevelopment shows the new paved embarcadero fronting the motel complex.

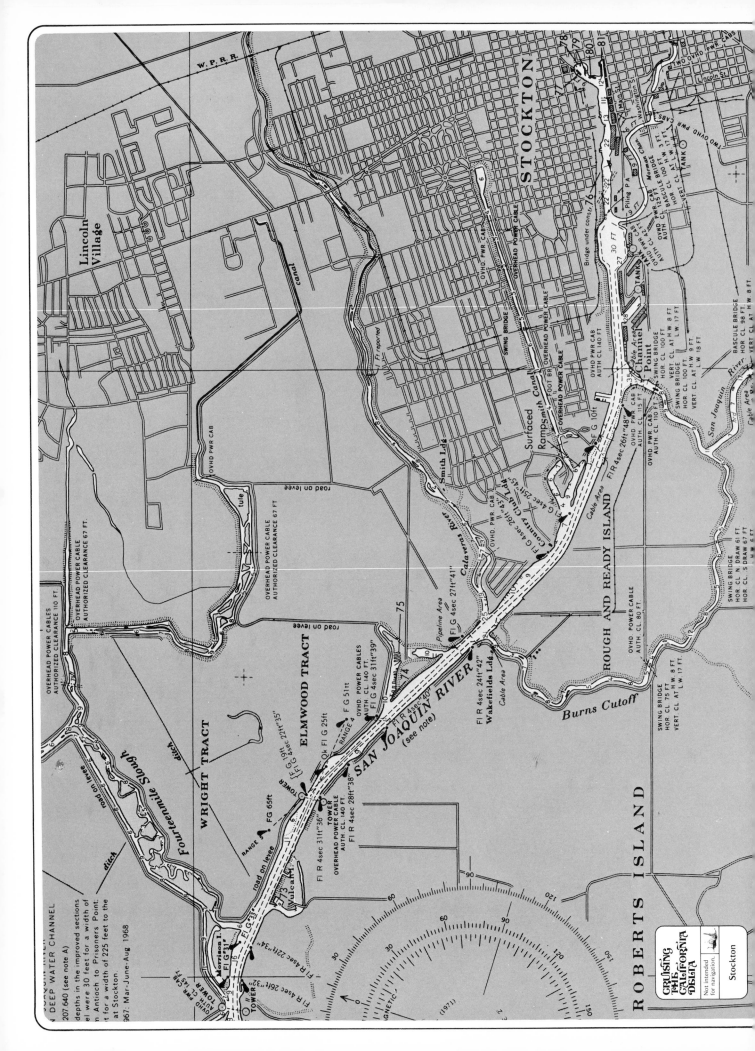

STOCKTON

LINCOLN VILLAGE

WRIGHT TRACT

ELMWOOD TRACT

ROBERTS ISLAND

ROUGH AND READY ISLAND

SAN JOAQUIN RIVER (see note)

Burns Cutoff

Calaveras River

Fourteenmile Slough

Smith Ldg.

Channel Point

canal

tule

W.P.R.R.

Overhead Power Cables
Authorized Clearance 110 FT.

Overhead Power Cable
Authorized Clearance 67 FT.

Overhead Power Cable
Authorized Clearance 67 FT.

OVHD PWR CAB

road on levee

road on levee

road on levee

OVHD. PWR. CAB.

OVHD. PWR CAB

OVHD PWR CAB

Overhead Power Cable
AUTH. CL. 140 FT.

Overhead Power Cables
AUTH CL. 140 FT.

Overhead Power Cable
AUTH. CL. 140 FT.

OVHD PWR CAB
AUTH CL. 115 FT.

OVHD PWR CAB
AUTH CL. 110 FT.

Overhead Power Cable
AUTH. CL. 80 FT.

OVHD PWR. CAB.
AUTH. CL. 3 FT.

OVHD. PWR. CAB
AUTH CL 100 FT.

OVHD PWR. CAB

TWO OVHD PWR CABS

TWO OVHD PWR CABS

DEEP WATER CHANNEL
207,640 (see note A)

depths in the improved sections
el were 30 feet for a width of
n Antioch to Prisoners Point:
t for a width of 225 feet to the
at Stockton.
967: Mar-June-Aug 1968

Vulcan I.

Morrison I.

TOWER

TOWER

TOWER
AUTH CL 140 FT

TOWER

RANGE

RANGE

Fl R 4sec 26ft "32"

Fl G 31"

Fl G 31"

Fl R 4sec 22ft "34"

Fl R 4sec 31ft "36"

Fl R 4sec 28ft "38"

Fl G 19ft 22ft "35"

Fl G 4sec 31ft "35"

Fl G 4sec 31ft "39"

Oc Fl G 25ft

F G 51ft

F G 65ft

Fl R 4sec 24ft "42"

Fl R 4sec 31ft "39"

Fl R 4sec 27ft "41"

Fl R 4sec 26ft "48"

Fl G 4sec 25ft

Fl G 4sec 26ft

Fl G 4sec 25ft

F G 10ft

Wakefields Ldg.

Country Club Ldg.

Pipeline Area

Cable Area

Cable Area

Pile
reported

Surfaced Ramp

Smith Canal

Foot Br

SWING BRIDGE

SWING BRIDGE
HOR CL 75 FT
VERT CL AT H.W. 8 FT.
L.W. 17 FT.

SWING BRIDGE
HOR CL N DRAW 61 FT
S DRAW 67 FT
HW 6 FT

SWING BRIDGE
HOR. CL 100 FT
VERT CL AT H.W. 8 FT
L.W. 17 FT

SWING BRIDGE
HOR. CL 98 FT.
VERT. CL AT H.W. 8 FT

BASCULE BRIDGE
HOR CL 100 FT
BASCULE CL 125 FT
VERT CL AT H.W. 9 FT
L.W. 18 FT

BASCULE BRIDGE

Bridge under const.

Piling PA

TANK

TANK

VERT. TANK

ditch

ditch

Fourteenmile ditch

Morrison Chan

Main St.

Washington St.

Lincoln St.

Channel

76

75

74

73

78
79
80
81

77

26
27
28

35

90

120

60

30

30

60

90

120

150

1971

MAGNETIC

The embarcadero around the Stockton yachting terminus is slowly being developed. Some major marina projects, now being planned by the city fathers, are expected to be built in the next several years so Stockton's future as a major pleasure boat port looks bright.

Stockton's riverside is recovering from the great waterfront fire of 1943 which burned the famed sternwheeler *Captain Weber*, destroying a valuable historical relic of the old riverboat days. The *Captain Weber* was featured in the films *Steamboat Round The Bend* and *Dixie;* Bing Crosby and Will Rogers were among the stars who trod her decks.

An exploration of the Delta should include some time in Stockton. The vacationing skipper has no excuse to miss it for he can take his boat within walking distance of this Delta city's downtown area.

A collection of Stockton's fine service and supply centers for yachtsmen. Top, left: Ladd's Stockton Marina on a bulge of the San Joaquin. Top, right: Looking toward Calcagno's and Habeeb's. Bottom, left: Near Ladd's is the Hoffman anchorage. A big launching ramp is between the two. Bottom, right: Stephens Brothers' retail store is near the famous Stockton shipyards.

Five Fingers

Five Fingers is the name yachtsmen have given to the five symmetrical harbors which lie side by side in a big tule island between Columbia Cut and Connection Slough, south of the San Joaquin.

The name is not on the official charts or the regional maps, nor do these even show the five cuts. This is surprising because these slots are much larger than many other harbor slots which are shown.

We did not know of them before a conversation with Spindrift Yacht Club members revealed their existence. This club stages an annual cruise and weekend raftup at Five Fingers. Members frequently gather there in their boats on regular weekends.

Bunty Lawless *moves into one of the big Fingers.*

16

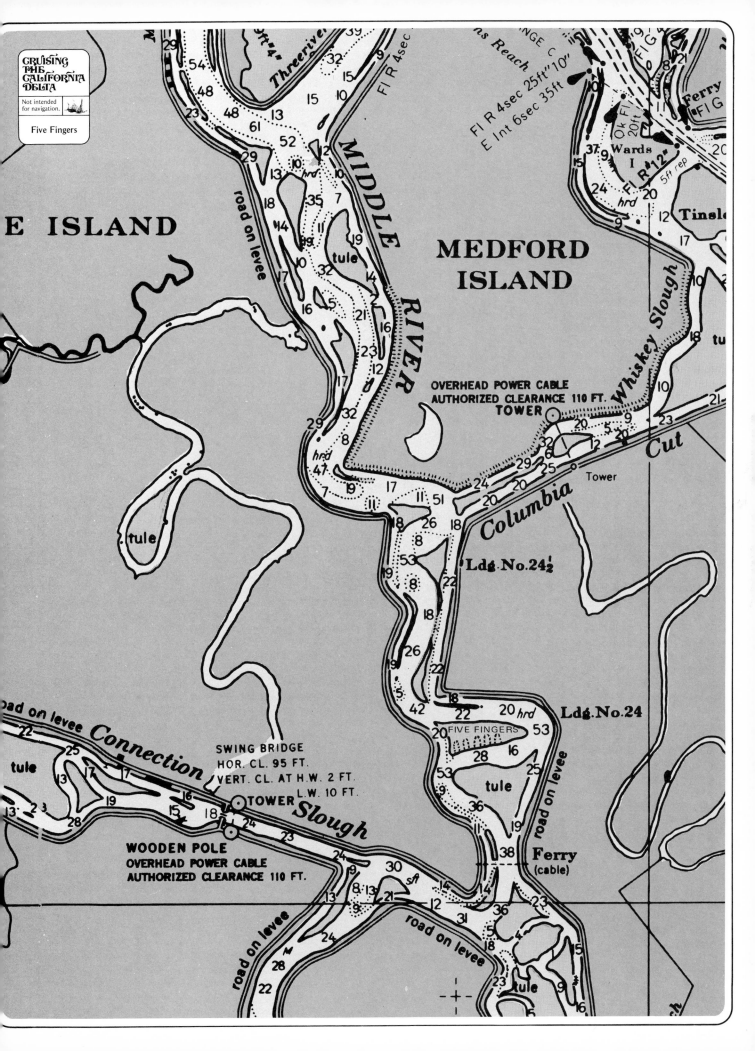

E ISLAND

MEDFORD
ISLAND

MIDDLE RIVER

Threerivers

Whiskey Slough

Wards I

Tinsle

Columbia Cut

OVERHEAD POWER CABLE
AUTHORIZED CLEARANCE 110 FT.
TOWER

Tower

Ldg. No. 24½

Ldg. No. 24

FIVE FINGERS

tule

tule

Connection

Slough

TOWER

SWING BRIDGE
HOR. CL. 95 FT.
VERT. CL. AT H.W. 2 FT.
L.W. 10 FT.

WOODEN POLE
OVERHEAD POWER CABLE
AUTHORIZED CLEARANCE 110 FT.

road on levee

road on levee

road on levee

road on levee

Ferry
(cable)

tule

tule

tule

We found the location delightful. Working south on Middle River, it is best to ride the east bank when leaving Columbia Cut astern. Depths run to 25 feet through this area. A big tule island looms laterally across a bend in the river. The rectangular harbors are on the south side of the first island, flanked by another big tule island. The harbors create several big protected estuaries. The normal breezes are shut out. There is one drawback. Some of the cuts are shallower than others and a skipper must consider tidal height and the depth of his keel in selecting his anchoring place.

The willows on the banks grow high, offering morning and evening shade. There is room for many boats in these unique notches. The shape and size of the indentations are impressive. They create quiet water and very pleasant surroundings.

An unproved legend claims that the Fingers were dug to create ports for the illegal importation of Chinese labor. The dug-out areas are shaped like barges and there would be room for small boats to take off Chinese if, indeed, smuggling was ever the business of Five Fingers. However, the story persists that this was a transfer point for hundreds of Chinese brought up from San Francisco and down from the railroad gangs to build the levees.

One of the several protected estuaries a few miles from Five Fingers. These provide good bases from which skippers can explore the cuts at leisure.

114

We have asked many people about this story and, while they can neither confirm nor deny it, they agree with my observation that so many barges trafficking in such an uncommonly large number of laborers would have been hard to keep secret. Instead, it is much more likely that soil and wet peat were dredged from these cuts and barged to levees in other areas. Anyway, the Chinese labor theory makes a good Jack London kind of tale. Regardless of the reason the digging was done, it has left a harbor bonanza for big yachts and small boats in the Delta country south of the San Joaquin. Pleasure-boating families all enjoy the Fingers.

Top: Enroute in to Five Fingers. Reaches here are wider and more open than those farther south. Bottom: A houseboat crew from one of the Fingers takes a break from waterskiing to explore adjacent harbors.

Top: The houseboat, tied up in one of the big Fingers, is mothership. The runabout provides local transportation. Bottom: From another houseboat, a crew member goes dinghy fishing along the low berm edges.

A Slough Named Disappointment

Disappointment's five mile course is punctuated with many small islands where boat clubs are acquiring vacation property.

People in boats will find plenty of lazy cruising, fishing, island retreats and places for fast boating along this slough that will not, despite its name, disappoint any crew.

The settler who found this slough to be a disappointment, and laid this undeserved judgment upon it when he named it, might have hoped to find a river rich in gold or a waterway to productive unclaimed farmland. By now, no one seems to know why or to whom Disappointment was a disappointment.

The slough is only five miles long. Cruising people do not seem to talk it up. Yachting traffic is not heavy. But those who will take time to explore its island waterways, devoting to it a short day's cruise or an overnight stay, will find Disappointment anything but disappointing.

Disappointment's course is punctuated with many intriguing small islands, thickly grown with trees and foliage. It is sufficiently open that its complex flow of waters is sun-specked in the riffles among the variations of deep green tones.

There are 18 islands in its short course, all of them fairly large. They are, in the main, soft triangle shapes,

17

flanked on either side by smaller dots of tules. The islands clog the middle of the slough and create a separate channel down each side of the course.

Snaking through midstream means following a maze of winding corridors, cool, narrow and attractive, with slow-moving currents. There are a number of crescent harbors and many lovely niches for the quiet anchoring of boats.

It is a treat to glimpse the occasional attractive summer homes, partly hidden from view by the trees and natural shrubs, each with its own private boat landing.

Several small-boat clubs from the cities of the lower valley are acquiring island sites on Disappointment for the vacation use of members. This is waterfowl country and there are many little club and private landings of the tree-limb and plank variety to be seen in the tule and grass thickets on the points of the islands.

If one goes up one levee and returns by the other, the scenery is varied and the length of the course, in effect, doubled to ten miles. Working all of the middle courses around the interesting islands is an entirely new project. We call this "port helm and starboard cruising," follow-

ing a graceful gliding path heightening the illusion that new scenes and extended distances are being covered. In our judgment, the middle of the slough is the prettiest.

There are several fine marinas: King Island Resort at the junction to White's Slough; Stan's Harbor nearby; Uncle Bobbie's Houseboat Haven and Paradise Point at the end near a big highway bridge and Bishop Cut. This cut is a straight, protected waterway ideal for off-the-main-course water-skiing. One of the large small-boat clubs is moving its valley headquarters to this vicinity and will hold water-skiing and racing events here. One word of caution: there are many snags and tule berms at the upper end making it difficult to work through Bishop and into White's Slough that way.

The interior tail of Disappointment Slough narrows and curls down into Fourteenmile Slough and, through Fourteenmile's thick, wide tule islands and very narrow waterways, on into the San Joaquin. The western end of Disappointment is considered its head and is near Tinsley and Wards islands. The main river wanders all over the land, forming a big double-pretzel shape. There are really three entrances into Disappointment from the San Joaquin. The tule islands are big and heavy with growth. They appear similar from the perspective of the ship's wheel. It is not uncommon to make several passes before one gets his full bearings. More than one skipper, initially feeling no need of chart and compass, has found himself cruising in ever-widening circles and a sea of frustration. However, there are no rocky dangers lurking beneath the surface and a little special attention to a chart solves the problem for those who are seeking their way down through the maze.

Left: Some action on Bishop Cut's straight protected waterway near Disappointment. Right: Paradise Point Marina has a good protected landing. There is fishing here and a sandwich shop.

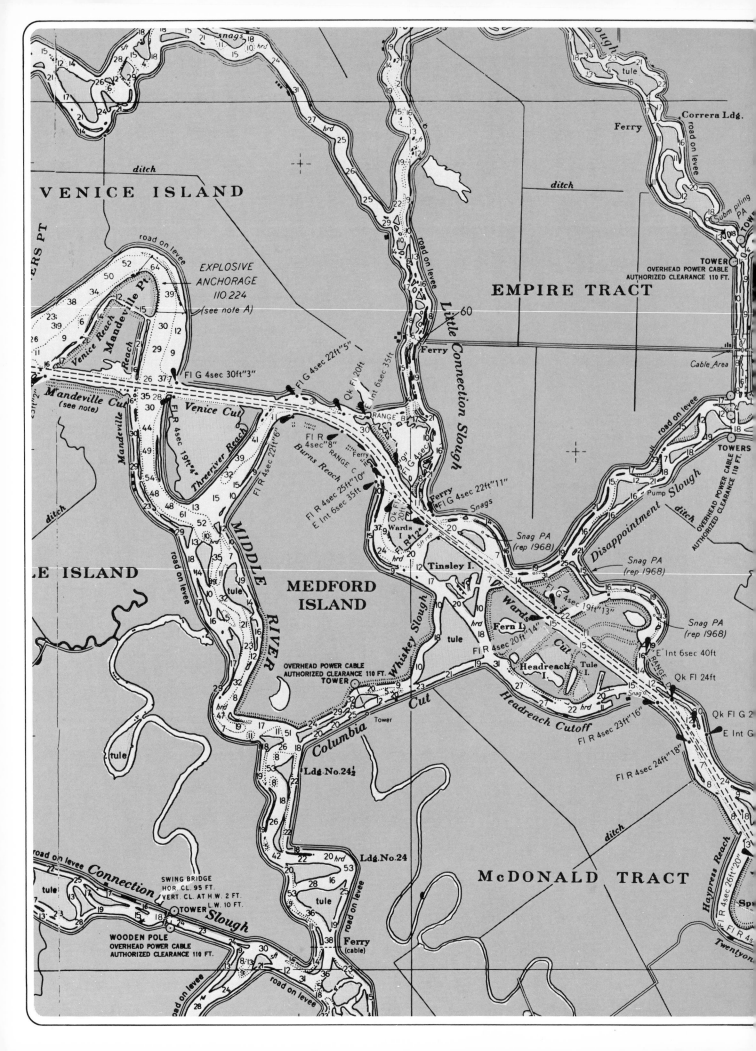

OVERHEAD POWER CABLE
AUTH CL 51 FT.

road on levee

ditch

KING ISLAND

Bishop Cut

WOODEN POLES

Telephone Cut

road on levee

OVERHEAD POWER CAB.
AUTH CL 26 FT.
FIXED BRIDGE
HOR. CL. 15 FT.
VERT. CL AT H.W. 3 FT.
L.W. 10 FT

BISHOP TRACT

ditch

OVHD. PWR. CAB.

SCALE 1:

NAUTICAL

To find SPEED, place one point of dividers on nautical miles run an
right point on 60 and left point will then indicate speed in knots.   Exam

STATUTE

YARD

1000   0   1000

ditch

road on levee

R CABLE
RANCE 110 FT.

ditch

Cable Area

SWING BRIDGE
HOR. CL. 74 FT.
VERT. CL. AT H.W. 3 FT.
L.W. 10 FT.

TOWERS
OVERHEAD POWER CABLE
AUTHORIZED CLEARANCE 110 FT.

ding

road on levee

road on levee   Ldg.

tule

tule

64

tule

tule

FIXED BRIDGE
HOR. CL. 36 FT.
VERT. CL. AT H.W. 17 FT.
L.W. 24 FT.

road on levee

OVHD. PWR. CAB.

Atlas Pt

road

OVHD. PWR. CAB.

ditch

ditch

SHIMA TRACT

Shima

ditch

road on levee

RINDGE   TRACT

SAN JOAQUIN RIVER
STOCKTON DEEP WATER CHANNEL

207.640 (see note A)

Controlling depths in the improved sections
of the channel were 30 feet for a width of
400 feet from Antioch to Prisoners Point;
thence 30 feet for a width of 225 feet to the
turning basin at Stockton.

Apr. 1967; Mar-June-Aug 1968

ditch

OVERHEAD POWER CABLES
AUTHORIZED CLEARANCE 110 FT.

OVERHEAD POWER CAB
AUTHORIZED CLEARANC

levee

Hog I.
Fl G 4sec 23ft "21"

Fl G 4sec 25ft "23"

Fl G 4sec 23ft "25"

Fl G 4sec 23ft "27"

Fl G 4sec 23ft "29"

Walters

Fl G "29"

OVHD PWR CAB
AUTH CL 145 FT
TOWER

Morrison I.
Fl G "31"

Fourteenmile Slough

ditch

WRIGHT TRACT

White Slough joins Disappointment through Honker Cut. With deeper water, it can be easily reached through Little Connection and Little Potato Sloughs. The two go well together and provide an interesting combination for a day of easy cruising. White is lined with pleasant farms and typical river scenery framed in old trees. White Slough is also thick with a number of wide tule islands; one island even has its own island within its own bay.

Near White Slough's big entrance is the home of the private Devil's Isle Club.

A number of fine marinas and sport fishing boat centers serve these sloughs. This area has been a fishing-party favorite for years.

More inviting island property,
privately developed, on Disappointment.

Bethel Island

Marine Center

Bethel Island is the Delta country's big-time marine center. Boating people do business up and down its sloughs in yacht sales, rentals, covered moorages and a host of allied services.

In simple, geographic terms, Bethel Island is another piece of lowland real estate among many. It is surrounded by slough water and rimmed by the Delta's typical mud and peat levees. Country roads and a connecting bridge to the statewide highway system of the "mainland" carry Bethel's resident population and visitors in and out to their homes, docks and boats.

Unlike the majority of other big Delta islands, Bethel is not an agricultural tract devoted to stands of asparagus, rows of corn, and orchards of peaches and nuts.

Bethel Island has developed into something special and vital for the yachting fraternity. Those familiar with it refer to it as the place that does all the yachting business. The island houses a thriving marine business community of about two dozen establishments, all thriving in an unlikely country setting.

Bethel Island's marina center is stashed away among surrounding sloughs, trees and rural roads. Many of the marine firms are not on the island itself, but face it from across the slough. Actually, Bethel's many covered boat stalls are usually easier to find by water than by road.

Bethel Island is also the home of two fine yacht clubs, the San Joaquin Yacht Club and the Caliente Isle Yacht Club. One clubhouse (the San Joaquin Y.C.) is mounted on top of a big barge stabilized on a river grid. The other (Caliente Y.C.) is on an island of rocks tossed up in the center of a slough and the only route between automobile and cockpit is via the club's ferrying system.

At the Bethel Island bridge by Sand Mound Slough.

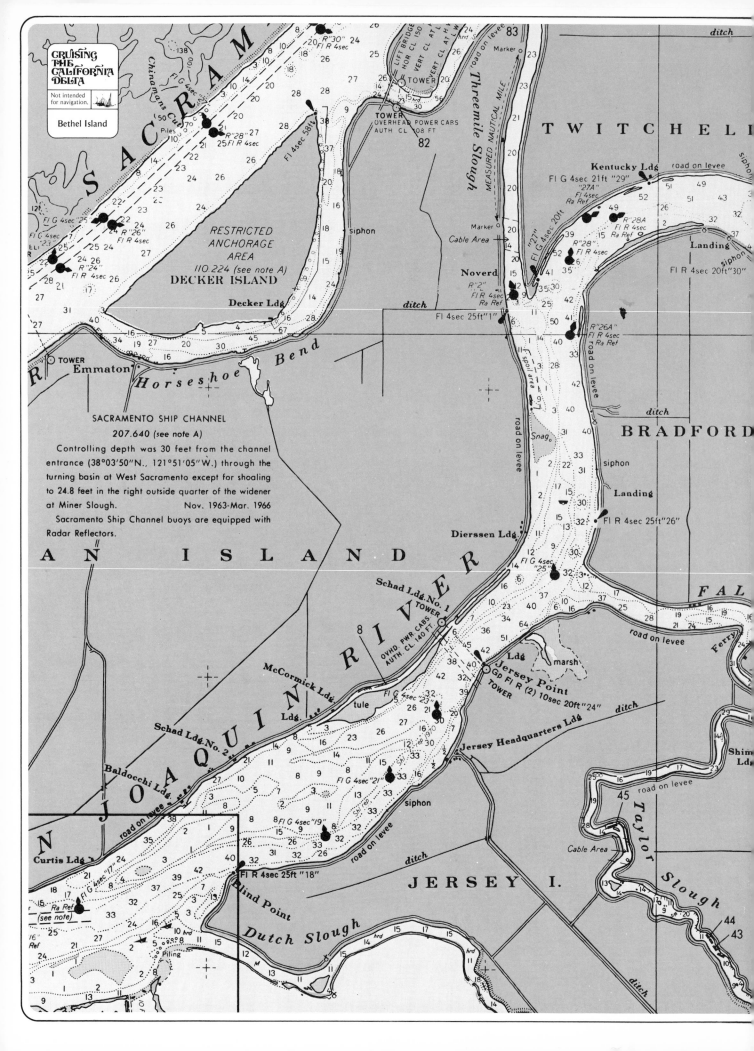

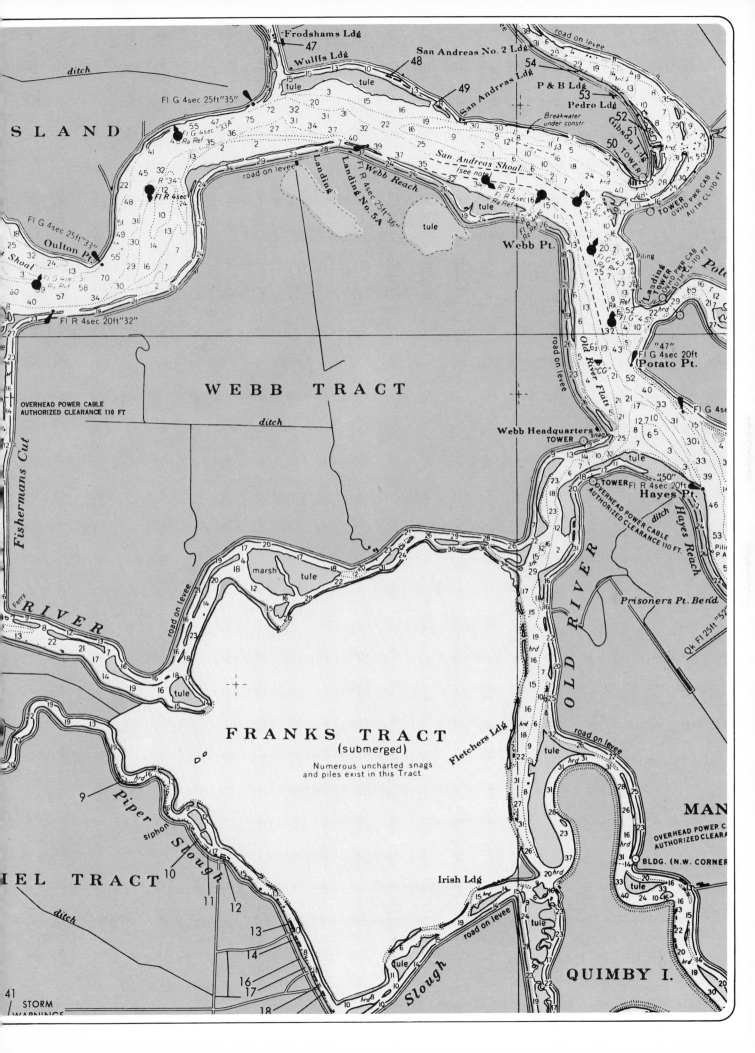

A Bethel Island circle tour will demonstrate the variety of shoreside property and the ingenuity of the owners. The circumference of the island is thickly dotted with homes, many of which are year-round residences.

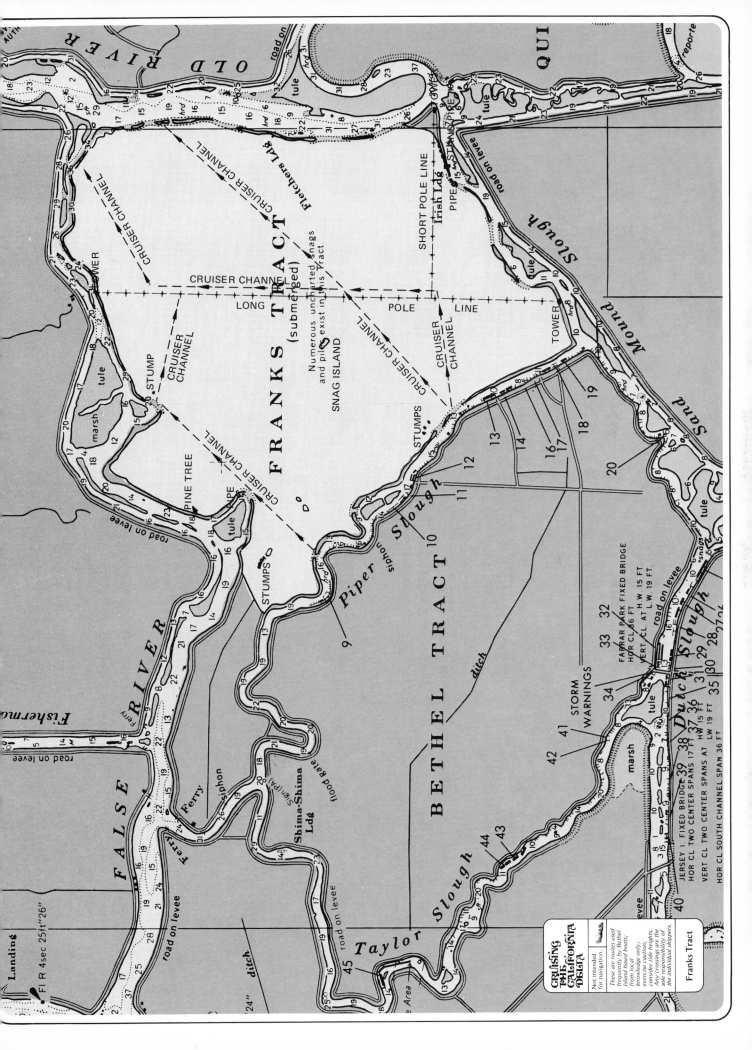

Bethel is the Delta's big time marine center.
Top: Bethel Harbor is an immense string of covered moorings reaching each way from the central building.
Center: Carter's houseboats and cruisers.
Bottom: River Queen cruisers offered for sale and rent.

Bethel Island's geographical position in the Delta scheme of waterways is happenstance, but it favors the travels of the peripatetic pleasure-boating people and sport fishermen. One can leave or enter any of the Bethel ports by at least six routes that extend to the San Joaquin River. Or, if one prefers, handy Old River, with its multiplicity of network miles to the south, is a route for cruisers going to and from Bethel.

Bethel's harbors are formed by long lines of floats laid against the levees. These are strung along three of the outer rims of its oval shape. This oval island is just over four miles in one direction and two-and-one-half in the other, but the water course around these three edges covers twelve miles.

Skippers and their crews can look and/or buy from a score of establishments handling fine yachts, small boats and motors. This is a center for houseboat sales and widely known for catering to the vacation visitors in the rentals of these floating motels for Delta cruising and fishing.

Bethel has launching facilities, crane haulouts and repair services. There are bait shops, marine equipment stores, boat-trailer yards, fuel facilities and all of the allied services that go along with the sale, service and operation of pleasure boats.

The island's circumference is also thickly dotted with homes in river-cottage style. Some of these cottages are year-around residences; many others are used as seasonal vacation homes. Most are constructed to just peek over the levee with gangways and stairs leading to little private landings. The backsides are tall structures which must reach up from the flat, low island terrain.

The cottages have acquired the patina of their river surroundings. They sit in a natural camouflage, blending with trees and the littoral of the diked river edges.

A pleasant cruising plan is to spend an easy day visiting Bethel's marinas and then circling the island's sloughs at slow speeds, allowing plenty of time for sightseeing.

This little full-circle trip allows one to appreciate fully the entire Bethel Island region, often neglected by boatmen arriving and departing on single courses. It is a slow trip because there are so many signs posting minimum speed limits. But then, sloughs move slowly; why shouldn't we?

Four sloughs are involved in the Bethel Island circling trip — Sand Mound, Piper, Taylor and Dutch sloughs. Sand Mound is crammed with tule islands. The reeds grow tall and one can easily confuse his directions.

There's a new kind of Bethel Island resident who prefers to have his home afloat.

Bethel has the advantage of good roads for those traveling by highway to their boats on the marine establishments. This is also good news for those trailing boats in for launching. Bethel is just a short distance off key highways 160 and 4, and an easy ride from Antioch, Tracy, Stockton and points beyond.

The island has another interesting feature. From its northeast side across Piper Slough lies the biggest lake in Delta land. This is Franks Tract on the charts—farmland totally covered by water and sometimes referred to as Franks Tract Lake.

This big, submerged farm went under in the thirties after two heavy winter seasons. In other chapters, we have described the cruising along the sloughs and rivers that rim the tract and are thinly set off by narrow strips of tule remaining from the old submerged levees.

Farm machinery, old buildings, trees, fence posts—they are all down there under the water ready to snag the unwary skipper. Those with no experience with the tract should avoid it. Commercial boat operators and some fishermen do use it. They know where to hunt out its deeper water and there has been an informal charting of shortcut courses across the tract.

The question is often asked about the possibilities of reclaiming this land. Reclamation would be a huge undertaking. Soil and probably rock for fill would have to be shipped from other areas.

Surveys have been made for a deepwater channel that would cut through the north side of the tract and link two sections of the San Joaquin. This would eliminate the need for ships to travel a big bend and would further shorten the distance to Stockton. The talk is that this will be done someday but no dates have been set.

The popularity and success of Bethel Island is a singular tribute to the imaginations and business acumen of the men who brought the marinas to the farmlands.

The ghosts of her captains and deckhands keep the Navajo's *bow on course but only irrigation water wets her garboard planks.*

Old Delta Riverboats
A Few Remain

No book about the Northern California Delta would be complete without a chapter on the old riverboats. And no vacation cruise of the Delta's waterways could give the visiting yachtsman the complete historic flavor of the region without at least a glimpse of one or two of the old vessels.

It is a pity that so few of the grand old riverboats remain to show the thousands of pleasure-boating families and visitors the principal characters in this colorful phase of the settling of the west. The toll by fires and sinkings, by conversions and at the hands of the wrecking contractors, has been inexorable among the paddlewheelers and the sternwheelers.

In a 70-year period, at least 250 river and bay steamboats were in Northern California freight and passenger commerce. This figure does not include the large number of steam-powered ferries that plied the waters of the San Francisco bay, though some of the riverboat hulls were later converted to ferry service.

At least 50 of the riverboats can be safely listed as side-paddlewheelers although an accurate figure might be as high as 75. The records are pitifully incomplete. Sternwheelers numbered around 140. Of the known propeller-driven single-enders there were only about a dozen.

Only one grand passenger riverboat was destined to survive and remain in the Delta as a full-fledged floating museum. Riverboat's Comin'!, Inc., an organization of Sacramento citizens, created the biggest steamboat news of the modern era in July, 1969. They hired a little 50-foot towboat and hooked onto the stern of the *Delta King* where she lay wasting away in Stockton Channel. Then they pulled her, paddle-end first, down the San Joaquin and up the Sacramento to a permanent berth on the river not far from the state capitol. The *Delta King* is at home now in a port she once served in her glory days.

This admirable civic move came none too soon. The old ship had been in Stockton for more than ten years while plans for her conversion failed, lawsuits accumulated and all attempts to utilize her historic elegance as a hotel and restaurant attraction ended in frustration. Much of her grand interior and fittings were plundered and defaced by irresponsible people who made their way aboard almost at will in the absence of a regular guard.

But on July 19, 1969, that sad chapter of her history ended and the *Delta King* made what will probably be her final river run. True, it was at the end of a towline, but more majestic days lay ahead. Now in her berth on the Sacramento, in the city of the same name, her 2,000-horsepower compound engines are stilled. Her giant paddlewheel sits somewhere in Cincinnati, Ohio, as a spare for her sister ship, the *Delta Queen.* But the old *Delta King* is afloat now in a new role not far from where gold was discovered on John Sutter's property.

Now that the *Delta King* is on display, even while they are still working to get her back in condition, there will be an increase in cruisers heading up the Sacramento from their harbors in the sloughs to visit the last of the great passenger ships still on the Delta. Much of her original luster has been damaged and lost but there will be plenty to fascinate her visitors after the rebuilding and restoring are completed. Of special interest is the old ship's propulsion machinery. The *King's* cranks are coupled with huge steel plates specially created for her in the great Krupp Works of Germany—a step vital to her operation. Prior to this, the great arms were coupled with forgings and these often failed. When this happened, broken cranks were sent on the fly, the vessel's structure was damaged and people were injured.

The *Delta King* and the *Delta Queen* were sister ships in service between San Francisco and Sacramento. For years the two passenger boats left on alternate evenings from San Francisco for Sacramento and made the return downstream the next night. Built in 1926 in Scotland, they were both towed across the Atlantic Ocean through the Panama Canal and up the west coast to San Francisco. The ships were 250 feet long with spacious decks and boasted the finest in interior finishes and stateroom fittings. The *Delta King* frequently carried 1,000 passengers a trip. But business began to fall off sharply in the 1930s when the paddlewheel era was nearing its end. In 1941 the two vessels were finally pulled from their scheduled runs about a month before the news of Pearl Harbor hit the west like a bomb. Life changed radically along the waterfronts. The government took over the *King* and *Queen,* attached a U.S.S. in front of their names and put them in service housing personnel.

Following their wartime service, a buyer had them scheduled for a return to passenger service on the east coast. But the *King* was picked up for housing at Alcoa's Kittimat Project in Alaska. The *Delta Queen* was towed back through the canal and established on the Mississippi River run where she attained new honors in keeping sternwheel steamboat travel alive. So, ultimately, both vessels were restored to useful roles in life.

There must be a bond of destiny between these two great ships. About the time the *Delta King* was successfully moved to Sacramento and was full of life with crews busy with her restoration and Sunday tours drawing thousands to see the progress, the U.S. Postal Service gave the *Delta Queen* a new assignment. They brought back an old tradition to the Mississippi—the steamboat mail service.

Steamboats were already carrying the bulk of U.S. mail when the first postal stamps were issued in 1847. Now the *Delta Queen* has been selected to reinstitute steamboat mail service and she will make many stops at famous old Mississippi river cities like Hannibal, Missouri. Adding one modern touch, the special mail pouches will be whisked to the local post offices on a motorcycle kept aboard the *Queen* for the purpose.

Resourcefulness has always been a characteristic of river people. In a blend of delight, daring and prudence, they seem always to find at least one new role for an old steamboat, even if it is by removing her steam boilers to power a sawmill.

In 1938, three old sternwheel steamboats were recommissioned, not to haul passengers again, but to save the huge, valuable farm tract on Mandeville Island from flooding. Getting one last, mighty effort out of three old Sacramento and San Joaquin river veterans typifies this kind of ingenuity born of a century and a half of settling the west and taming its rivers.

Mandeville Island ·sits in a triangle formed by Old River, Middle River and the San Joaquin. The fertile fields are sub-level. Though the land was covered deep with water, more was needed to force it out than could be obtained from pumps. The levees were reinforced and dams were built across the breaks.

The owners then picked up three riverboats—the long-idle *J.D. Peters* of 206 feet, the *Reform*, of equivalent size, and the most famous of the three, the huge 252-foot Southern Pacific "liner," the *Navajo*. The *Navajo* had ended her S.P. years of service in 1918. The steamboats, all with their big stern paddles churning, were run through a gap and into the island's infield lake. There they were strategically located and anchored. The dam was replaced and the boilers were fired for around the clock service. With the paddlewheels facing huge wooden sluice boxes that carried over the levees, the last ever full-steam-ahead order was issued for each and the waters were forced out. These three may be the only steamboats in history to paddle themselves into a farm field berth and the only ones to have squash and potato stalks, rather than tule grass, brushing at their waterlines.

The 252-foot Navajo *is the spectre ship of the Mandeville Island farmlands.*

Here, from top are before and after shots of the old Sutter, *first as a river freighter on her Sacramento run; now as John Moore's popular Riverboat Restaurant on the lower Mokelumne. At bottom is the* Sugar Barge, *another old river freighter converted to a new role.*

The huge *Navajo* still rests there though the *J.D. Peters* and the *Reform* are gone. Her paddle bay is empty and her bow turned away from Old River. She is a forlorn sight until one stands in a furrow of rich soil near her bow and looks skyward to her high, square wheelhouse. Then, with the blue sky above, she takes on a bit of her old majestic look. Orders will never be shouted down again to the men standing ready to handle her lines and capstans. Only the sounds of cooing pigeons are heard from the open pilothouse windows. But she, with her companion ships, had a moment of final glory in the struggle to preserve Mandeville Island's rich farmlands.

The old *Sausalito* was a famous San Francisco ferry rather than a regular Delta carrier, but her preservation and conversion at Antioch into a fine clubhouse is commendable. Her story has its place in the ensuing chapter about the Delta yacht clubs.

The old *Sutter* was a plain Jane river freight boat plying the Sacramento and San Joaquin. A mere 156-footer, she was the kind that wouldn't get a second glance when the *Delta King* or the *Capital City*, with their grand fittings, were in port. Any hardwoods that might have been mounted along her cargo decks were never rubbed and varnished. Instead they were roughed and scuffed and hell-for-stout to absorb the jostlings of the freight she carried between the river cities and the rural landings.

But changing eras can create unexpected destinies for cast-aside hulls. The old *Sutter*, a name not to be confused with the early-day *Captain Sutter* sidewheeler, now operates eight months of the year on a schedule that "carries" more passengers than any of her palatial floating rivals ticketed in their later years. Yet, though the *Sutter* is afloat, she never leaves her landing on the west bank of the lower Mokelumne.

When the little freighter was the *Sutter*, the name was painted in small letters on her grubby bow. Now she is a floating eating house with entertainment. A long sign stretches across her texas deck and its light bulb letters proclaim her as "Moore's Riverboat Restaurant."

The old *Sutter* didn't carry ticketed passengers so there was no fancy dining saloon to be noted for its cuisine. But there is now. And she is also now appropriately noted for her buffet situated near the transom. "Buffet" was the early name given by the river folk to the bar or space on the passenger boats where the high potency proofs were poured from the fancy bottles, a service that was particularly appreciated on trips when there was a cold bite in the damp of the tule fogs.

More people recognize the *Sutter*'s white enamel deck house today than ever paid attention to her during her original career. Her present, spacious social hall is busy. And, in fact, she is one of a very few old riverboats remaining in any form of active service.

The *Sutter*, as John Moore's Riverboat Restaurant, has marina floats for visiting pleasure boaters who can board by way of the port gangway. The parking lot is on the vessel's starboard side and connects with the levee road that runs adjacent to B&W Resort, Perry's, Korth's Pirate Lair and Spindrift.

The two gangways adjust to the tidal height and lead into a large, athwartship passageway that once accommodated a freight elevator moving between the deck and the high river warehouses and landings. This entry also leads to the companionway into the dining hall.

John Moore, the owner, is now the *Sutter*'s captain. He has shown imagination in building the old freighter into a Delta attraction and a better looking ship than she ever was in her youth. In addition, Moore's successful project saved a piece of Delta history for posterity.

Moore did all of his own planning and much of the carpentry during the five years it took to complete the rebuilding. The main deck opened for business in 1966. The Riverboat Restaurant's backbar houses a fine display of interesting old photos of other Delta ships. Automatic bilge pumps keep the bilges emptied. Along with the refrigerating equipment, the pumps are the only machinery operating between the old ship's 4- by 12-inch frames and 4-inch-thick planks. The *Sutter* was not a steamboat. Her twin Atlas direct-reversing engines are still in place in the engine hold. These engines are of the same type that powered the diesel auto ferries of a few years ago. When changing directions with this type of equipment, the engineer shuts off the diesel fuel, there is a pause as the ship moves steadily toward the slip, then a bang as compressed air is shot into the chambers and the diesel, in reverse, takes hold.

In the engine room now, the old engines sit in the middle of dozens of canisters with their tubing running topside to supply the carbonated beverages for the barkeeps—an ingenious use of the space.

Moore has performed a real service in preserving the old *Sutter* as one of the few remaining riverboats available to the public view.

Pleasure boaters cruising the Bethel Island area will find another old freight boat that has been stationed for years on Piper Slough. It is a snack-shop operation where one can snub his pleasure boat against the old freighter rub rails and board for a bite to eat or to have a drink.

The old *Marin* was on the Sacramento at Garcia Bend for years as a river restaurant but she has been removed from the scene. We were not able to find where she might be now—if indeed she still exists in any form.

So the toll of the old riverboats has been great and precious few remain. Almost all of the 250 steamboats and a number of diesel-powered river freighters are gone. Some ended by fire, some by sinking, some were converted to ferries and others gutted for the plebeian service of barging. Their historic steering wheels and items of brass fittings have disappeared or are widely scattered.

Aware of all this, the Sacramento community's decision to get into action and save the *Delta King* is highly commendable. It is fitting that some kind of steamboat museum room with a library of photographs and the histories of her predecessors should be brought together in her house.

And, as we have related, the old *Navajo*, the oldest of the remaining steamers, is now on private farm land at Mandeville Island. Perhaps she could be salvaged still, through public subscription and served by a public landing, so boating people could view the exterior of this venerable old steamboat of early Delta and San Francisco history.

To save the best of what is left of the old riverboats, restore them to their former grand condition and make them available to the public seems to us to be a very worthwhile project for the people who love the California Delta, residents and visitors alike.

Meanwhile, thanks to the people working on the *Delta King* project in Sacramento—and men like John Moore—there are still one or two places where we can show our youngsters a prime example of the riverboat glory days in California.

Down Among
the Tules

The Delta Yacht Clubs

The Sacramento Yacht Club is the river area's oldest organized boating group.

This is the story of the Delta yacht clubs, associations and groups with weekend island, slough and river sanctuaries. In this outback of land sunk between several thousand miles of water, with great farms everywhere and more boating visitors than there are resident regulars, one hardly expects yacht clubs to be flowering among the tules. But there they are—in considerable number and variety.

The growth of the permanent population of pleasure hulls in Delta country has been exceptionally strong. The barometer for this can be read in the list of yacht clubs and formal boating organizations now in existence there. In their organizational structure there is considerable variety and color. There are over 20 Delta boating organizations. Eighteen of these belong to the prestigious Pacific Inter-Club Yacht Association of Northern California. The balance are the specialty groups and clubs whose members already belong to other major yacht clubs outside the area.

This large development of clubs out in a vacation-oriented rural area is extraordinary. One's first time, casual impression of the Delta is one of countrified remoteness. The only large congregations of people seem to be on the fringes of the farmland region where the cities sprawl. Only in these cities does one expect to find the Delta yacht clubs, following the established pattern of the rest of the west coast where the clubs are located in waterside cities of both small and large dimensions.

*The San Joaquin Yacht Club
on Dutch Slough is a converted barge.*

No one is astonished to find a formally structured yacht club in Sacramento, Stockton or Antioch, and perhaps a few other towns. But the fact that there are over 20 fine organizations, all active with hulls afloat in many of the marina harbors, in this Delta heartland farm country is astonishing. Even this figure does not take into account the boating clubs in the Sacramento and San Joaquin valley towns. Many of these unregistered, unlisted clubs maintain their own Delta holiday retreats. In fact, a number of these clubs, largely made up of members with trailerable hulls, are moving to establish their own permanent Delta headquarters.

It is logical to ask where do they all come from—these boat owners who keep 3,000-plus fine craft regularly on Delta waters under covered moorings. The answer lies in their membership rosters. The owner/members live all over California. They, with their families, are yachting commuters who prefer to spend much of their boating time in what they all call "My Delta."

These boating people, for all of their activities at sea and on the big waters elsewhere, also enjoy the more subdued pleasures of the river country. They soon find themselves deeply attached to it. They begin to look for a second home and a port for their boats where they can relax with friends away from the pressures of the cities. Tinsley Island's development as the summer port of the world-famous St. Francis Yacht Club of San Francisco came about this way.

Tinsley is a little island halfway between Antioch and Stockton. One side of the island faces the San Joaquin River ship channel at Wards Cut. The rest of the island forms a big curving shoreline on a quiet, levee-lined estuary. This estuary used to be one of the river's meandering main channels until the work of the dredges sequestered it by carrying the commerce through a straight-line cut elsewhere. This work left an isolated and protected channel of charm, free of the commercial traffic.

Tinsley is a good-sized island on the charts but "Tinsley Island" to the pleasure boaters has come to mean the magnificent private development of the southeast section. There the notches and tule berms create a series of hidden harbors for the use of the St. Francis Yacht Club members. There are fine landings and large grassy malls for volleyball, bocce ball and baseball games. Overlooking the whole development is an old time- and water-worn San Francisco Bay lighthouse with its light tower. The lighthouse was transported to this site on Tinsley by barge, a hefty undertaking by club members.

The St. Francis club purchased the island in 1959 for the summer use of its members. In the fall, they host the famous Tinsley Island stag affair. Yachting people gather at Tinsley from all over the world for an invitational meeting that follows a week of racing on San Francisco Bay. Their Tinsley Island program, now in its fifteenth year, provides a year-long committee activity for the St. Francis club men.

At Antioch, the Sportsmen (Inc.) Yacht Club, which elected its first Commodore back in 1931, has a particularly appropriate Delta headquarters. Its clubhouse is a converted 236-foot sidewheel steamboat ferry, the old *Sausalito*, which plied those same waters that the St. Francis club's lighthouse once flooded with light.

In 1930 this Antioch group of yachtsmen and sportsmen purchased the ferry after she ended her career of crisscrossing the bay. She had been in the ferry service on the bay since 1884. The *Sausalito* was a colorful ship that was dear to the hearts of millions of San Francisco Bay commuters. The Antioch club's action gave her new life in the role of a clubhouse and thereby preserved her profile, saving her from the wrecking crews. Today the old *Sausalito* serves a hundred-member yacht club.

The former *Sausalito*'s boilers were removed to make room for the construction of private cabins on the lower deck for member-families, a clever idea in vacation housing and one where a cabin is truly a cabin. The club's meeting hall and ballroom is on the upper deck, flanked by a restaurant and bar. The bar is an historic item in itself. This structure of wood, brass and glass was one of the cocktail bars at the 1939 World's Fair on Treasure Island in San Francisco Bay.

The Delta Yacht Club property is near Tinsley and shares the other end of a meandering branch of the San Joaquin. This club development, on what was once a heaped-up old tule island, is a whistle toot from the San Joaquin River's ocean-going commerce, yet is a delightful, pastoral shoreside retreat.

The Delta Yacht Club members locate her as being in the vicinity of navigational light No. 14. This is the regular club site for members who live in such scattered cities as San Jose, Mill Valley, Oakland, Modesto and other parts of Northern California. Considering that the property is at quite a distance from most members' homes, the place is maintained on a rather grand scale. The modern mooring floats come close to setting a record for frontal length. The nearby skyline of the stately poplar trees is reflected in the shimmering water and provides shade when the fleet is in. Her 1971 commodore, William H. Gray, Jr., said of the club's Delta location: "Our site is one of beauty, a refuge for us all without crowds and the attendant problems. We may be social or withdrawn, as we wish, and we preserve this fine characteristic of the club by limiting membership totals."

The club is the outgrowth of an informal association of boating people who came together in 1938 and incorporated under the Delta Yacht Club in 1941. On an island everything must be brought in by water. In earlier years, the houses and floats were towed in at the start of the season and out at the end of it. Eventually, the present caretaker's house was brought in by barge and was used as the clubhouse until 1954 at which time the new clubhouse arrived—also by barge. In 1957 a filtration system was installed and it is no longer necessary to tank in fresh water by boat.

Their floating dock facilities have been expanded several times and the present array, on styrofoam flotation units, is 650 feet long. The dredged out lagoon on the other side of the island has 20 berths accommodating boats to 65 feet. There is a fine swimming pool, rest rooms and showers, lawns, playgrounds and outdoor cooking and picnic areas. Altogether it is a wonderful blend of yacht club and resort.

The San Joaquin Yacht Club is not the largest in California. Its building, on its property at Bethel Island, is within sight of those traveling the highway bridge and is limited in size. But members boast that since the club has owned the present facility "it has logged more time at sea than any other Delta yacht club."

This club first operated at the San Joaquin harbor in Antioch, the place that gave it a name. Now it is located on Dutch Slough. The formative years were the early 1950s at the Antioch location. A reorganization was effected in 1949 and the site moved to Bethel. There were 20 members. From there the history of the club's problems and disappointments with the new property reads like a treatise on why the loyal members should have jettisoned the movement. But they didn't and, in 1954, they purchased their barge with its two-story superstructure. It was probably a boarding facility for men at Mare Island. The decks were rough and the barge was in need of considerable work. "It would have made 'Hogan's Goat' look like a precision facility," is the way Past Commodore Richard Salsman describes the acquisition. With the backing of 45 members, the barge was towed to its present site from Vallejo and an enormous conversion project got underway. A fine commercial galley, rich paneling and hardwood floors were installed. Berthing floats for 40 cruisers filled the waterside and a dozen other major improvements earned it the nickname of "the floating Hilton."

But wooden hulls need underwater attention and big barges can't be hauled out on Delta ways. The wags of other clubs were soon calling it the "sinking Hilton." The expensive decision was made to put her on piles but the leaking clubhouse had to be towed to Antioch while her permanent grid was being built. The seams opened up and disaster was barely averted. Salvage operations were undertaken. Large, steel flotation tanks were worked under the barge and pumps were brought into action. In late 1962 the floating, ubiquitous San Joaquin Yacht Club was again on the end of a towline, homeward bound to Bethel. At the end of the tow, she was secured in place on her permanent base of piling and structure and the 22-year struggle to establish a yacht club was successfully concluded.

The Cruiser Haven Yacht Club landing in the Brentwood area on an unusually quiet day.

The yacht crews gather at the Spindrift Marina, home of the Spindrift Yacht Club.

Marina life is the new compelling force in the Delta and fine establishments are everywhere. The percentage of covered moorages filled by boats that can be floated under the roofs is judged to be as high as 90 percent of the total resident Delta fleet. The neighborliness of marina life leads to close associations among boaters and new yacht clubs sometimes have their beginnings in the marina boating neighborhoods. Spindrift Yacht Club, with 75 powerboat owning members, is one of these clubs that evolved from its marina associations. The club is located at Harry Schilling's Spindrift Marina on a sheltered slough on the San Joaquin close to the Mokelumne entrance. Founded in 1965, it soon acquired the lower floor of the Spindrift restaurant building as its clubhouse and has since moved forward with an interior building program. The club features group cruising to Delta ports.

Bridge Marina Yacht Club started up in 1952 near the Antioch bridge under similar circumstances. As it grew, its 150 member-families reached the big day in early 1968 when they opened their own clubhouse. The clubhouse is located on pilings in a harbor area on the edge of the San Joaquin River close to its juncture with the Sacramento. BYMC is a gateway club. From its favored location one may elect to travel the Delta on either the San Joaquin or the Sacramento since these two great rivers meet close to the club headquarters. In addition, member boats have a short convenient run to San Francisco Bay where they can participate in the many yachting activities going on in that locale. Opening Day Parade on the lower San Joaquin begins and ends at BYMC. This is a cruising club with high participation in Over-the-Bottom and Predicted Log cruiser racing.

The Mokelumne Yacht Club began simply as friendly, informal gatherings of yachtsmen from other clubs downriver who would leave their boats over instead of making the long water-trek home after a pleasant weekend of Delta boating. Originally they called themselves the "No No Club" because they countenanced no rules and had no officers, no burgees, no dues and no meetings. But they found themselves so active as a group, having so much fun porting their boats on the Delta, they became the "Yes Yes Club" and incorporated the Mokelumne Yacht Club with all of the formal rules and trappings. The B & W yacht harbor became their home base and meeting place. There are 80 active members now. MYC belongs to the major yachting associations and has a heavy interest in Coast Guard Auxiliary activities. Many members serve regularly in Delta patrol work. The club's founding precepts include promoting yachting interest in the Delta, championing good seamanship and safety and maintaining a membership that is rated high in proficiency in boat handling.

Devil's Isle, a specialty club formation, has a fine facility along White Slough, not far from Little Potato Slough. Devil's Isle is a Delta club for the members of a power squadron who have formalized yacht club affiliations elsewhere. In the early 1960s Ted Clark, of Lafayette, began cruising the Delta region in earnest. Finally he decided he would acquire a piece of island property for a vacation port. He searched for an island with the right sun exposure and a good harbor area. As it happened, Clark was also very active in the Diablo Power Squadron and had served as its public information officer. When Clark found the excellent property along White Slough, he realized that many of his squadron associates were showing keen interest in his project. With his power squadron associates, his personal plan expanded and the concept of forming a club where friends could cruise together, an association that would be enhanced by a mutual interest in U.S.P.S. activities, was born. An invitation was extended to squadron members and enthusiastically accepted. Under Clark's leadership labor, material and funds came together in a group effort by squadron members and Clark realized he was drawing on an amazing pool of talent, skills and enthusiasm. By 1963 the group had constructed their outstanding headquarters as a center for their cruising, fishing, squadron and vacation activities. The Diablo Power Squadron probably is the only single power squadron membership that figured out a way to own its own Delta island. At the dedication of the club this plaque was mounted: "From bits and scraps, plus time and effort, all donated by Diablo Power Squadron members for their fun and frolic, this patch of tule materialized. Please protect it."

In the Delta environment one does not expect to find a big rock island in the middle of a slough. About the only natural material around that is harder than silt is dried peat. But there is a rock pile island right in the middle of Taylor Slough along the western shore of Bethel Island. And this unlikely rock has a clubhouse on it, landings around it, and a double row of covered moorings attached to it and reaching up the slough like a giant rudder.

This is the Caliente Isle Yacht Club, the only one with slough waters flowing around it on all sides forming a natural moat. The members park their autos behind a high dike, walk up and over to the landing and jingle the bell for "bum boat" service to the clubhouse landing.

Caliente grew up through the past decade under the guidance of Sam Martin, of Oakland, whose cruiser, *Dry Martini*, is active from the Bay to the Delta. The club is known for its power cruiser racing and has a string of outstanding victories in this specialty. The members enjoy being on the island and find that it promotes close fellowship. The galley is run on a cooperative arrangement. There are 70 cruisers in the CIYC fleet and a long waiting list that has prompted plans for more berths and a clubhouse extension.

Not including the private clubs who maintain Delta property for vacation activities, there are 18 Delta-based yacht clubs incorporated in the formal manner and participating in the activities of yachting associations. The pleasure boats involved lean very heavily to the power cruiser classifications because the Delta is cruising and fishing country. Gung-ho sailing and racing is limited by the narrow waterways and the rather special Delta slough environment.

Of these 18 clubs, eight were organized in the 1960s at the same time that Delta ports were bulging with this new, permanent pleasure-boating expansion. Fourteen of the 18 yacht clubs were organized after wartime gasoline restrictions were lifted in 1945. Only four of these present clubs existed prior to 1941.

The fine Sacramento Yacht Club, rich in river tradition with a clubhouse right at the river level, elected its first commodore in 1929. It has a dozen sailboats in its fleet and around 70 cruisers. The clubhouse is another fascinating building, double-decked on a huge barge, its back to the state capitol building, and its front to one of the few fully navigable, famous rivers running through the middle of a major city.

But this isn't the only "YC" activity in Sacramento. The city also is headquarters for the Fort Sutter Yacht Club (1949) and the River View Yacht Club (1956). The Fort Sutter Yacht Club, one of the older Delta clubs, is a very active cruising club. Commodore Roy Beach explains they are a Sacramento yacht club but many of the members berth their yachts at Willow Berm Marina near Isleton and use the marina as their informal Delta headquarters.

The Stockton Yacht Club filled an early need on the other side of the Delta and is only a few months younger than the Sacramento club. The Stockton club has carried on an equally fine tradition. The SYC clubhouse is on a high knoll. Its exceptionally fine grounds, with grand old trees filtering its view, slope to its boathouse facilities on the north bank of the Calaveras River. Club members are justifiably proud of the impressive, restful setting.

Powerboating dominates the Delta even though hundreds of bay sailors find time for cruising. But the Stockton Sailing Club, operating since 1946, is the one group keeping the windward-leeward fun out front. There are ten major class fleets within the club and three dozen boats in assorted classes of limited number within each class. Weekend racing is spirited and the club is very active.

The city of Stockton also shelters the Weber Point Yacht Club so the two major Delta cities are matched with three yacht clubs each and lead all others.

Back in the glory days of sliding gangplanks, puffing stacks and turning paddlewheels, Rio Vista was a bustling river town midway on the Sacramento River be-

Deep in the lagoon at the St. Francis Yacht Club's Tinsley Island retreat—the San Francisco club's Delta facility.

tween the state capital and San Francisco. All of the fast boats stopped at Rio Vista, a key point with a Mississippi-town kind of heritage. The town waterfront still carries some of the marks. But the bollard has been replaced by the yacht-float cleat downstream a couple of miles where all of Rio Vista's boating is now centered at a beautiful marina. Typical of the rest of the major boating centers, there is a yacht club, the Delta Marina Yacht Club, founded in 1964. DMYC has a basic fleet of more than 50 power cruisers. Its membership has been drawn from the west around Walnut Creek and as far as Menlo Park, from the south as far as Fresno plus a dozen or more from Sacramento. The improved, new river roads let the skippers get from widely scattered homes to the heart of Delta cruising and fishing with ease.

Yacht clubs like Diablo (1961) have been born out of mutual desires of their boat owners to be as close as possible to the routes and pleasant potentials of interior river cruising. To call any one of the clubs typical is difficult because each really goes its own way. But DYC is representative of the current high levels of group boating activity that have caused Delta pleasure boating to expand so far beyond the potential of its own sparse, local populations.

DYC's enthusiastic membership resides from near Oakland to the warm valley suburban cities over the mountain ridges to the east—and toward the Delta highways. With their headquarters at Bethel Island, handy to the highway, they are superbly located for taking off into the thousand miles of waterways in any direction. DYC skippers and their families are first and foremost cruising people, with keen interests also in fishing and waterskiing.

DYC members enjoy the days when their anchors are deep in the mud of some off-corner tidal harbor. Like their counterparts who enjoy cruising in Catalina harbors or British Columbia's stony refuges, they particularly like to discover the little-known private places. When they can slide those devil-mask pennons on their bows into a good one, theirs are kingly roles enjoying their private preserves.

All cruising people who know of little places not yet discovered by the crowds like to keep their finds to themselves.

Skippers use some devilishly clever devices and formulas, when on the air, to beckon friends without sending others foraging on the chart tables. It is the same game that the fishermen play to protect that special spot where the fish are striking.

"Our skippers enjoy quiet coves," explains one of DYC's officers. "We while away the hours visiting, swimming, sunbathing and working on our boats. We have our own names for these places so we can call friends on the radio suggesting they meet us without having a dozen others cruising in to see if we have a better spot than the one they are heading for. We have three favorites.

"Our 'Shhh Slough' is on the San Joaquin—a small break in the tules where we pass through into a deadend waterway a half-mile long and extremely quiet. There we are ignored by hundreds. We anchor bow and stern. There is a beach where we can stand in the water for hull work, painting and varnishing—no wakes, no dust.

"The cove we call 'Cocktail Haven' has the cleanest and warmest water around. It is hidden behind small islands. The entrance is a tricky one to negotiate but once inside the water is deep and clear. It will accommodate 20 cruisers and is our favorite harbor for rafting-up. There is no access to the shore.

"The 'Ron-de-vous' is a lake formed by dredging but the entrance is shoaled in. During a spring runoff a small fleet of our cruisers worked our props while the tide was dropping from very high water and we blew out a ten-foot-wide channel deepened to five feet."

As the seasons roll on, these clubs enjoy the best of river life in this agricultural valley of very warm summers and delightfully pleasant springs and falls. The winters are mild in comparison to other parts of the country and are, at most, plagued by recurring tule fogs but by little else. Group cruising is the most popular activity.

At Antioch, the Dos Rios YC was formed in 1961. They selected a name that would reflect cruising life on and around their two big rivers. The club's swallow-tail burgee is designed to depict the merging of the Sacramento and San Joaquin rivers. Because this is also a group cruising kind of club, it was decided it would accumulate no real estate, hold club expenses to a minimum and channel all its functions into cruising activities out on the Delta and away from home port.

Cruiser Haven Yacht Club is based near the Brentwood area and is located farthest south of this group of major Delta clubs. CHYC was incorporated in 1959. They maintain an excellent waterside mooring property for the membership. Their members are drawn largely from the Oakland area, from the peninsula cities south of San Francisco and from the suburban valley east of the Oakland hills.

The farthest club to the west, a kind of downriver anchored group, is the Pittsburg Yacht Club, which is located near the stretch of waters where the two famous rivers, Sacramento and San Joaquin, meet and merge. PYC is a veteran club, launched in 1949.

The fleet boats of these major yacht clubs are numerically but a small part of the thousands of pleasure boats that embark upon the Delta waters each summer, coming from near and far, by highway and by waterway. Yet, as it is with the rest of the west coast boating fraternity, these organized clubs are pace setters in the level of activity and the tempo of Delta pleasure boating. Many visiting yachts arrive carrying club affiliations from all over the coast adding to the large number and variety of club burgees being flown in the Delta. In fact, if there were such a thing as a guest book at the river portals, on any given day it would reflect the spread of yacht clubs throughout the world as well as almost every one of our own fifty states.

We cannot close this chapter on the Delta yacht clubs without telling the story of one of the most famous of the specialty clubs—Grindstone Joe's Association.

This group is not of standard yacht club structure. Like its near neighbor, the Devil's Isle specialty club, it is not a formal yachting club with membership in the prestigious Pacific Inter-Club Yacht Association of Northern California. But it is one of the most colorful groups of pleasure boaters ever to hoist a burgee. The story of the club's beginning has been told many times. But if we purport to give you the whole of the Delta, we must include it here. It is really the story of a man and a rowboat that came to rest on a tule island in Little Potato Slough in Delta country almost 40 years ago.

The Caliente Isle Yacht Club sits in the middle of Taylor Slough on a rock island all its own.

In the depression days of the 1930s, Joe Attello, an old salt quite worthy of this rugged rating, decided he would seek contentment and a less harried existence for his partial retirement years by finding on the Delta a garden spot bordering his own harbor.

For years, Joe had been eking out a meager living as net fisherman. He used a rowboat over the same courses on San Francisco Bay where young Jack London, 40 years earlier, had sailed his *Razzle Dazzle* out into the dark nights and swift currents as a freebooting, fighting, hard-drinking oyster pirate.

This decision of Joe's to locate his own anchorage on the Delta led him and hundreds of eventual boating friends over a long trail of years that culminated in the formation of the most extraordinary yachting club and club facility in existence. Joe Attello's is now a very lovely, peaceful section of property, adorned much of the year by beautiful hulls at anchorage. The club facility deserves all the reverence it attracts as the enduring monument to the story of the late years of the life of Grindstone Joe. His place, its history, Joe's own story and the earthy distinctiveness of the club name, belong in any chapter purporting to tell the story of the Delta yacht clubs, conventional and unconventional.

Joe Attello had not yet participated in the incident of the grindstone, from which he acquired his distinctive name, when he gathered up his partner and a few belongings and left Vallejo in his rowboat. He rowed far up into the San Joaquin River and its tributary sloughs, searching for that remote island home where he could fish and grub out a modest but independent livelihood from the rich Delta soil.

Joe had not been raised on the Delta, as was the case with so many of the old characters who lived along the sloughs and rivers. He was born in the 1880s in Chile near the Strait of Magellan and joined the Chilean navy when only eleven years old. When out of this service, he emigrated, still a young man, to the United States. Without the skills for the civilian life in his new country, he went into the trade he knew best by joining our navy.

After his navy service, Joe made his way to San Francisco where he worked as a fisherman on the bay, a tough lonely figure in his rowboat, tending the nets with his huge calloused hands. But Joe had a dream and he felt he could best realize it in Delta river country. So Joe, with his partner, went up into the Delta to find his place. He found a little tule island with a protected bay there that seemed to him to fit the dream. So he went to

work, with his partner, to build his cabin and his landing, clear the land and put in his gardens.

Pleasure-boat cruising in the thirties was limited and skippers using the Delta got to know almost everyone who lived ashore along the waterways. In swinging around Joe's tule outcropping near Bouldin Island, often using its quiet waters for an anchorage, they were attracted to Joe's industriousness as he improved his rural surroundings. Most of these yachtsmen were up from the San Francisco clubs, but there were others from the Delta cities, too. Strong friendships were formed with Joe.

One day in the off season when none of them was around, Joe rowed off on a trip for supplies and left his partner to care for the place. Joe had been busy fishing, clearing land, constructing shelters and floats and cutting wood. In all this activity his grindstone, which had been hard to come by, played a major role and was essential for the sharpening of his tools and knives. However it happened, avoidable or otherwise, the partner somehow broke the stone. When Joe returned, he was angered over the accident. An argument ensued. Too much was said and Joe's partner took off with his belongings.

Joe brooded over the loss, not of the partner but of the grindstone. It was a heavy loss to him with his projects ahead and a decided lack of money. To make his point, in a final venting of his wrath, he hoisted the broken stone onto the roof of his cabin for everyone to see. The strange exhibit gave him many opportunities to explain his side of the quarrel. His boating guests heard Joe's version a number of times. They wouldn't have been a bunch of fun-loving yachtsmen, worthy of their cult, if they hadn't come up eventually with the name of "Grindstone" for their beloved Joe. And the name stuck—to both Joe and his place.

The harbor at Grindstone Joe's Association in Little Potato Slough.

The men who knew him well agree that he was a river character, an eccentric, but a man with great character, admired and respected for his essential honesty, loyalty and courage.

Joe was very industrious and very proud of his developing property. In spite of his age, he single-handedly beautified his island. It was a major project. He planted trees and gardens and brought hundreds of wheelbarrow loads of peat mud from the stream to build the rustic lane that he lined with poplars. The tall lovely trees Joe planted distinguish and beautify the large, protected bay today. No line of trees adds more to a protected yachting harbor than this great stand of stately poplars, made all the more imposing after one has reached it through the flatter Delta country and Little Potato Slough.

Strong friendships grew between Grindstone Joe and this informal group of yachtsmen who, with their boats, visited him regularly. He made them welcome. Gradually, he improved the landings. As this became a regular stopping place for them, their voluntary payments to Joe became a major source of his meager income. A club of sorts was coming together. Joe was fussy about this clientele and the men to whom he allowed the privileges of his island and port. Due to his selectiveness, stemming naturally from his years at sea that had taught him to recognize character in men, his group of about 60 boat owners was a blue-ribbon one of respected industrialists, businessmen and outstanding Corinthians.

Joe built a special barbecue for parties ashore. This is still in use today along with the great poplar-lined lane he constructed with the river-bottom soil. Legend has it that Joe got along best with powerboat families and disliked sailboat skippers. This has been refuted by many who were closest to him, saying it was simply too far from the main ports for sailboats to come up often and that it was just by chance that some of the men Joe barred from his island happened to be sailboat skippers. However it was, for his chosen few Joe gradually built bigger and finer floats and gangways. Grindstone Joe's became a very popular gathering place for the elected.

Joe was a devoted lover of dogs and he cared for many, including three beautiful collies. His favorite collie was Baby. When Baby died, Joe erected a headstone at the grave with this epitaph: "Baby was a good dog. One of the best here takes a rest."

Well, Joe was one of the best, too. When he passed on, this cruising fraternity that he had gathered about him through his offering simple, honest friendship to visitors, joined together to obtain his property. They formed a corporation for the preservation of the island area. It was given the name of Grindstone Joe's Association to honor an old sailor from Chile who had left them a legacy of trees and roses, a beautiful harbor, a good philosophy of life and one of the finest ports away from home in all the Delta.

To end a chapter on Delta yacht clubs with the story of Grindstone Joe's seems very suitable.

There are more fine private groups in the Delta, like Grindstone Joe's and the Devil's Isle group, whose members belong to major formally organized yacht clubs outside the area. But the list of Delta yacht clubs that follows is limited to those clubs, formally structured, who are members of the PICYA-the Pacific Inter-Club Yacht Association of Northern California.

The Delta Yacht Clubs

(This list of Delta Yacht Clubs is limited to those that are members of the Pacific Inter-Club Yacht Association of Northern California. There are, as mentioned in our Delta yacht club chapter, many fine small private clubs in the area who are not PICYA members and, consequently, are not listed here.)

BRIDGE MARINA YACHT CLUB
Route 1, Box 524
Antioch 94509

CALIENTE ISLE YACHT CLUB
Bethel Island 94511

CRUISER HAVEN YACHT CLUB
Route 1, Box 99-A
Brentwood 94513

DELTA YACHT CLUB
Tule Island
Stockton 95206

DELTA MARINA YACHT CLUB
P. O. Box 75
100 Marina Drive
Rio Vista 94571

DIABLO YACHT CLUB
P.O. Box 348
Bethel Island 94511

DOS RIOS YACHT CLUB
Route 1, Box 515
Antioch 94909

FORT SUTTER YACHT CLUB
c/o R. Beach, Commodore
1931 Florin Road
Sacramento 95822

MOKELUMNE YACHT CLUB
Route 1, Box 52
Isleton 95641

PITTSBURG YACHT CLUB
Pittsburg 94565

RIVER VIEW YACHT CLUB
P.O. Box 2624
Sacramento 95812

SACRAMENTO YACHT CLUB
Foot of Broadway
P.O. Box 2428
Sacramento 95811

SAN JOAQUIN YACHT CLUB
P.O. Box 326
Bethel Island 94511

SPINDRIFT YACHT CLUB
P.O. Box 67-P
Isleton 95641

SPORTSMEN, Inc. YACHT CLUB
Route 1, Box 565
Antioch 94509

STOCKTON SAILING CLUB
P.O. Box 1661
Stockton 95201

STOCKTON YACHT CLUB
3235 River Drive
Stockton 95204

WEBER POINT YACHT CLUB
North Spud Island
River Mail
Stockton 95206

Boating In
For Dining Out

Giusti's at Walnut Grove was founded around the turn of the century.

There's good eating to be had in the California Delta. Local residents are justifiably proud of the history, traditions of hospitality and the fine cuisine of their restaurants. Visitors to the region should not conclude their trips without treating themselves to as many Delta dining out experiences as time and the vacation budget permit.

Pleasure boaters will be particularly pleased at the variety and number of these restaurants that are easily accessible by water. You can literally boat in to dine out in the Delta and the log of your cruises there will not be complete without at least a half dozen or so of your own personal reports on the crew's dining out expeditions.

Many a first mate feels the less time spent in the galley, the more enjoyable the cruise! The skipper will be apt to agree if they are exploring the Delta. The area's restaurants are inevitably associated with the fine old riverboat traditions of good food and hospitality. Their menus have obviously profited from their waterway connections with San Francisco and that city's great and deserved reputation for fine dining.

Residents will protest that if the visitor has not taken a meal in each and every one of the traditional favorites, he will have missed the total of the Delta. This understandable regional loyalty seems particularly strong and prevalent among the local yachtsmen. The feeling probably stems from the days when Delta pleasure boaters were fewer in number, really good pleasure-boating facilities were few and far between, and a good find in a restaurant accessible by boat was a status symbol jealously guarded by the gourmet skipper.

21

Today the Delta restaurant brigade, by boat and auto, is a large one and the list of eating places offering very acceptable to superb food is long and growing. But in their decor, their western hospitality, their informality in dress contrasting with their insistence on quality and authenticity, even the newest additions to the Delta restaurants list demonstrate pride in the regional history.

The tradition of good restaurants and the feeling that they should be patronized often, and appreciated, seems to have a strong affinity with the Gold Rush days and early Northern California history. The riches of the western seas and the soils were blended to their ultimate goodness through the influences of European cookery, the best of the northeastern part of this continent, and the influx of the Oriental. The excellent results of this mix of recipes and menus spread through the regions of Northern California and onto the great riverboats. These vessels were beginning to acquire considerable social status along with their reputation for providing the mundane service of necessary transportation.

These famous old steamships were caught up in this tradition of good food because their captains and owner companies had to stay financially healthy in the face of vigorous, imaginative competition. Just as with the great Atlantic passenger carriers, many customers made their choices at the ticket windows only after comparing the pleasures of the dining rooms and the warmth of comradeship at the bars. The bars on the old ships offered lavish buffets which rivaled the dining salon menus.

The Delta restaurants of today that carry on these traditions and are products of this heritage are the darlings of the pleasure fleets. People also travel long distances by auto to sample the eating houses on the levees. Landlubbers seem to enjoy hobnobbing with the elite off the decks. The pleasure boaters are always properly attired for their evenings out, wearing what is locally known as the "tule tuxedo"—yacht jacket and cap, shorts or denim slacks, a knit tee shirt and deck shoes.

The choice of restaurants in the California Delta is as varied as the distances required to reach them by boat or auto. It would be impossible to mention all the Delta restaurants in this or any other book. One problem is the continual growth of the list of the available eating places. New and interesting restaurants are being opened every season. The visiting Delta yachtsman of tomorrow will want to log his own four-star eateries and make his own discoveries. He and his crew will have their favorites but I and my crew have ours. We will share a few of them with you in some little detail and then, in the Delta directory section at the end of this book, we will list as many of the cruising area restaurants as we could locate by press time. And we will even leave some extra space for you to log in your own additions to the list.

And so—all ashore who's going ashore—to eat!

Giusti's (pronounced Jee-oo-stees), at Walnut Grove, is the oldest of the well-known Delta restaurants. It was founded around the turn of the century by a grand gentleman, the father Giusti, who believed in serving with pride the best foods produced by the surrounding region. His wife, Irene, served with him and she continued the operation of the restaurant after his death. Their daughter, Dolores, and her husband now carry on the family tradition of good food and good service on the same site and in the same buildings. Dolores Giusti married Manuel Morias, "Mo" to everyone in the Delta. Today, the efforts of Dolores and Mo Morias and the members of their family make Giusti's one of the still-reigning favorites. The dining room is small. The best of the foods from the nearby ranches is still the mainstay of the menu. Giusti's is known for its great steaks, salads and exceptional mushrooms. The classic old bar is quiet with old shoe decorum until weekend and holiday nights when the boating crowds line the place to share a convivial drink, eat and visit with friends. There are excellent mooring floats and a good fuel service at the restaurant's guest dock.

Giusti's was a favorite of the late Erle Stanley Gardner who, in later years, adopted the Delta as his friendliest cruising place in the world, and set down his informal meanderings in the area into three separate books. In one of them, *The World of Water*, Gardner wrote of Giusti's: "In the fertile soil of the Delta country are gardens which grow crisp and tasty vegetables, and these vegetables in turn find their way into salads for Giusti's customers. It is impossible adequately to describe the warmth of the place, the impression of hospitality, the cool crispness of the salads or the flavor of the food. Many commercial resorts extend service on the basis of 'Hello, Sucker! Come on in and be fleeced. We're as glad to have you as a kid is to entertain Santa Claus. But up at Giusti's there is warm friendliness, a genuine desire to accommodate. That atmosphere emanates from people who are happy with their lot in life and want you to be happy, too."

The Point restaurant and cocktail lounge is part of Jack Baumann's excellent, modern, boating harbor complex. It takes its name from its location on a point of land overlooking a vast sweep of the lower Sacramento River, downstream from the historic river port of Rio Vista. This point also commands the channel entry into the Delta Marina, the only modern yachting harbor in this lower reach of the River of Gold. Diners may watch the movements of the big ships and the barge traffic, the yachts in and out of harbor, and the private fishing boats doing well with stripers, salmon and catfish. The steaks, roasts and seafoods are on a par with big-city restaurants. The broiled salmon is an enticing specialty. The Point plays host to large gatherings of crews from group cruises and, reflecting the owner's dual hobbies, there is a courtesy bus that brings civilian flyers in from the local airport.

Foster's Bighorn is located in downtown Rio Vista. Times change and Foster's Bighorn does not draw the yachting crowd as it formerly did. Presently, this is more of a landlubber's restaurant. But Foster's is a must for my family crew, not only for the food but for the decor. The place is like a big game hunter's museum. William ("Bill") Foster, the founder, was an intrepid big game hunter with outstanding talents for collecting and displaying the mounted heads of his trophies. The main dining area and the bar, both separate from the coffee shop, are lined with these historic displays from a lifetime of hunting all over the world. The trophies range from the tiny heads of gazelles to huge elephant heads bearing enormous tusks. We recommend Foster's as a place for good casual eating and fascinating sightseeing.

Jack Baumann's Point Restaurant at the Delta Marina in Rio Vista overlooks the Sacramento river traffic. At top is the restaurant; below is a diner's view from the marina side. The Point commands the channel entry into the Delta marina.

146

"Al, the Wop's" is what every Delta skipper has called it for years. Most of them roll it together with the touch of long familiarity and it comes out "Alawops." But its formal name appears on a small painted sign hanging over the sidewalk along the "street of overhanging porches" in the Chinese town of Locke. The correct name is **Al's Place.** This is an historic saloon and steak house. The original Italian Al's path took him through a bit of Delta bootlegging into the highly respectable restaurant business, or so the story goes. When he opened the doors of Al's Place, he was the only Caucasian businessman on the Chinese-dominated street. Al's is now a part of Locke's history and a part of Delta restaurant history. The old place has high ceilings, a long bar of dense, soft, beautiful mahogany, a reputation for big steaks that can be seen cooking on the range just abaft the bar, and walls lined with old signs, geegaws and antiquities. Al's is different, a side street experience and the traditions have been carried on by its present owners. The restaurant is also noted for the dollar bills stuck to the 20-foot-high ceiling, a trick that is performed by the proprietor when the guest hands over his bill. Unfortunately, there are no landings at Locke and yachtsmen, thus handicapped, do not go to Al's Place as often as they might if there were a handy, nearby harbor. But we urge a meal at Al the Wop's, combining this experience with a sightseeing trip down the old Oriental-west streets of the historic town.

The Steamboater, Walnut Grove, is located on Steamboat Slough just above the River Mansion. It enjoys one of the choicest Delta settings because it leans out from a very high levee, overlooks the famous anchorages for yachts along the treed banks on the other side of the slough, and also commands a panorama of yachts and deluxe small boats plying famous Steamboat. The restaurant can be reached by levee road. This is one of the newer Delta dining places, quite modern with a nautical touch to its decor. We enjoy the bar and also rate it a first-class restaurant. The house has several culinary specialties from which to choose.

Al's Place (top) is down this street in the old Chinese town of Locke. The Steamboaters (bottom) is one of the newer Delta restaurants. Diners there have a sweeping view of the pleasure boating on Steamboat Slough.

John **Moore's Riverboat Restaurant,** at Moore's Yacht Haven on the lower Mokelumne, is the classic conversion/restoration of a gunky old diesel-powered river freighter. The job done in converting her is truly magnificent and the old *Sutter* is very attractive in her modern role.

The big riverboat floats and also has large guest floats for visiting yachts. John presides over each evening's festivities in his yachting blues and cap and the relatively new, but fast becoming famous Delta restaurant and bar dominates the restaurant scene on the lower Mokelumne. The Riverboat may also be reached by levee road. There is a huge parking area; gangways lead from waterside and shoreside through the foc'sle of the old boat. Nightly entertainment and dancing are offered the Riverboat's guests in the best tradition of the old showboats. The Riverboat is another of the places where the convivial yachtsmen like best to gather. The menu features steaks, seafood and prime rib.

The Spindrift restaurant peeks over the levee onto Schillings Spindrift Marina. It is located on a protected shoreline slough fed by the San Joaquin, not far from the Mokelumne and the string of marinas from Korth's to Willow Berm. The restaurant serves Friday, Saturday and Sunday during the main seasons and is rated very high for its seafood and an excellent salad bar. The interior of the Spindrift is the most nautical of them all in its furnishings which are highlighted throughout with ship's wheels, running lights, and the repeated use of marlinspike rope, line and knot-work strung to blocks, deadeyes and belaying pins. There's a delightful cocktail lounge here.

The **Riverview Lodge** restaurant at Antioch stands high above the river on pilings, with its dining room picture window facing a grand riverscape where the San Joaquin and Sacramento rivers meet. This is an excellent dining place on the old Antioch riverfront and it is reachable by both the main highways and the waterways. Riverview Lodge specializes in seafood dinners but I can also recommend the prime rib and the steaks are reputed to be excellent. Diners can watch both freighter and yacht activity on the water below while they enjoy the Lodge's culinary triumphs.

At Petri's Yacht Harbor in Antioch, the fine center owned and operated by Angelo Petri (of the renowned California wine family), a new interesting restaurant is making its debut in the spring of 1972. We have a stop here scheduled for our first Delta cruise this summer and, from all reports, we have a delightful dining experience in store for us at **Petri's.** The restaurant was still without a name when this book went to the printer.

Lovely **Tiki Lagun** is situated on Turner Cut off the Stockton deepwater channel. It is a small restaurant, a favorite with Delta pleasure boaters who enjoy its soft river setting. The restaurant is part of a fine resort. The surroundings are lovely and well maintained. A neighboring diesel ferry constantly crosses the cut in front of Tiki Lagun in its chugging work of connecting levee highways. The menu is, as you would suspect from the name, studded with the house's South Sea island and Hawaiian dishes and the decor carries out the South Pacific theme.

Bethel Island is a Delta gourmet's paradise. Many fine restaurants are located here and some of our happiest dinner ashore experiences in the Delta were logged in when we were cruising the stretches of water in this area. At Bethel Island itself, among places popular with those with small boats and large yachts, **Boyd's Harbor** is known for its hearty breakfasts and general coffee shop and cafe service. Owners here plan an interesting expansion starting in 1972.

The **Sugar Barge,** the old converted freighter facing Franks Tract, opened in 1972 under new ownership. The Sugar Barge is one of the few old floating hulls left anywhere now being restored to a new role in life as a Bethel Island restaurant. House specialties are steak and prawns.

The popular **Boat House Lounge** is a Bethel Island dinner restaurant with a huge bar built around a boat hull design—nautical decor with hatch cover tables for diners. They have dining and dancing and are one of the new attractions that fits well into the old standby list of the island favorites. Try the lobster here.

The Chinese restaurants of the Delta mustn't be missed. There are several and most of them are good. We have a favorite of our own—Bernie's, located at Isleton.

Bernie's Chinese fare is at its best when a reservation is made with Bernie in advance. Be sure there is more than one couple in the party. Tell Bernie what you like but let him suggest several dishes to be shared by your party. Most of Bernie's regulars say "Bernie, we'll leave it up to you." Do the same and you won't regret it.

Then there are the Mexican restaurants—another natural outgrowth of the Delta farmland history. There are several fine places with a south-of-the-border cuisine. One of the newest of these is **The San Andreas** restaurant at Happy Harbor, an old mooring under new development, near the Spindrift. At the San Andreas, Al and Del Garcia are rated very high by the cruising crowd for their wonderful, authentic Mexican dishes. They also feature Mexican and American style breakfasts for boaters and are becoming known for their great start-of-the-day menus.

The Walnut Grove Marina's Snack Barge is a place where one can boat in, get a table on the broad deck and watch the boat traffic on Snodgrass.

If you have a large party and you want to eat outdoors, contact the **Lost Isles Club.** They will host your group and the food will be both ample and delicious. Lost Isles Club has an interesting, attractive harbor with a restaurant and bar catering to the boaters-in. The place is located off the Stockton deepwater channel almost at Turners Cut.

The best breakfast in the Delta, for our money, is served in the coffee shop at **Korth's Pirate Lair Marina.** They take special pride in their breakfast menu and there's no better way I can think of to start your cruising day if you are in the lower Mokelumne stretches of the Delta, near Willow Berm.

Over at the New Hope Landing, east of Giusti's, at **Wimpy's New Hope Cafe,** the casual dining is from the second floor. Diners overlook a constant small-boat parade in the summer time. Both food and location are excellent. Dinner steaks are the specialty of the house.

In the line of buffets, we have been sent to the **Del Rio Hotel** in Isleton and rate it well.

In Stockton, within loud-hailer distance of Uptown Marina and Calcagno's yacht harbor, the new **Holiday Inn** that looks down on the harbor development of the city is a drawing card for boat crews dining ashore.

And so the list goes on and on.

There are many other drop-in places. The small-boat clan can raise a landing in the quest of a hamburger as casually as the man behind an auto wheel.

There is one thing for sure—if this piece has missed some deserving favorites—and it undoubtedly has—some Delta skipper will be telling the other boats about it and no place and no one will be missed for long. In California's Delta, amongst her pleasure-boating crews, the number three topic after cruising and fishing is the restaurant that, in the judgment of the skippers, really rings the ship's bell.

Directory of Delta Boating Facilities

This directory of Delta facilities available to the pleasure-boating family is intended as a guide for newcomers and a reference for those revisiting the area. The list is fairly long. Skipper and crew can enjoy the Delta's many miles of secluded waterways and still never be far away from marinas and shops ready to supply their vacationing needs.

Landings, fuel docks and launching facilities; stores selling fishing supplies; boat rental agencies; boatyards, dry docks and marine centers for emergency repairs; campsites for families who want to stay ashore; a choice of eating places ranging from snack bars to gourmet restaurants—all these await the cruising family in the Northern California Delta.

Houseboats—popular and practical for family vacations on Delta waterways—may be rented in the area. Since rental agencies receive hundreds of reservation requests each year, it is suggested that plans for houseboat cruising be made well in advance. Information on fourteen of the Delta's leading houseboat rental firms may be obtained by writing the Secretary, Houseboat Owners Association, Route 1, Box 514, Antioch, California 94509. Those seeking information should be specific in stating their requirements, giving family needs, vacation dates, preference in areas and other pertinent facts.

We have tried to make this directory of Delta cruising facilities as complete and current as possible. But do keep in mind the Delta area is growing very fast. And growth means change. Even in the length of time it took for this book to be printed, there were undoubtedly some new facilities that opened up, some that acquired new owners and/or new names, some that expanded their services. Also, though we tried to list every facility in the categories we covered, we undoubtedly missed a few! To increase its value to the individual skipper, and enable him to compensate for any errors and omissions, we have left space for logging in personal discoveries and making notes for future reference.

For convenience in locating facilities, we have divided the Delta roughly into six areas: Antioch and vicinity; Bethel Island; Stockton and the south Delta; Rio Vista, Isleton and Terminous area; Walnut Grove-Courtland area; Clarksburg-Sacramento area. Mailing addresses are given as an aid to pre-vacation planning.

Most of the facilities listed here are on the water or within easy walking distance for the yachtsman. Facilities not directly on the water are identified in the listings with asterisks. With this directory, and charts and maps of the area at hand, plan ahead for your next cruise in the Delta.

Antioch Area

The first area encountered on entering the vast Delta complex from Suisun Bay is the Antioch region of the middle Delta. Its borders extend from Montezuma and Collinsville in the northwest to include most of Decker and Sherman islands, half of Jersey Island, and the cities of Oakley, Pittsburg, Brentwood and their environs. In the center of the area is the junction of the Sacramento and San Joaquin rivers and the city of Antioch, the western gateway to the Delta. Besides the 10-mile stretches of the Sacramento and San Joaquin, the area contains Dutch Slough, Broad Slough, Sherman Lake and Big Break which surround Kimball, West, Browns and Winter islands.

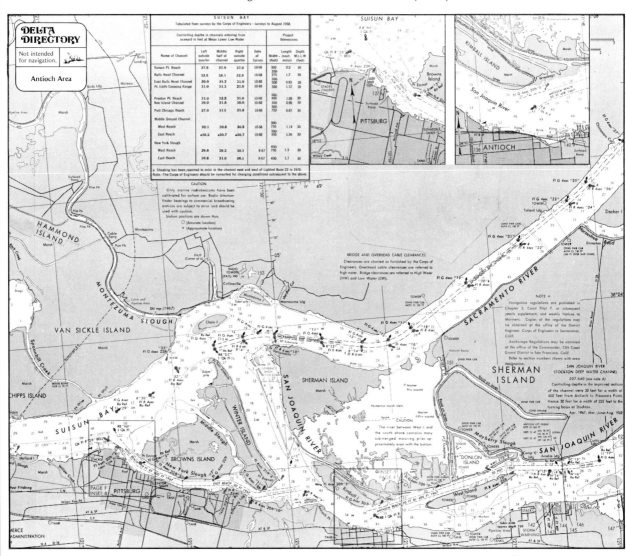

Camping

Collinsville Fishing Resort
Star Rt. 283, Box 125
Suisun

New Orwood Resort
Rt. 1, Box 88
Brentwood

Pittsburg Yacht Harbor
5 Cutter St.
Pittsburg

Sam's Harbor
Rt. 2, Box 333
Oakley

Dining

Bale's Bait Shop
Rt. 1, Box 500
Antioch

Big Break Resort
P.O. Box 171
Oakley

Collinsville Fishing Resort
Star Rt. 283, Box 125
Suisun

Delta Marine Center
111 Fulton Shipyard Rd.
Antioch

New Orwood Resort
Rt. 1, Box 88
Brentwood

Petri's Yacht Harbor Restaurant
Rt. 1, Box 542
Antioch

Pittsburg Yacht Harbor
5 Cutter St.
Pittsburg

Riverview Lodge
Foot of H St.
Antioch

Tommy's Antioch Yacht Harbor
P.O. Box 756
Antioch

Fishing Supplies

Bale's Bait Shop
Rt. 1, Box 500
Antioch

Bob's Bait Box & Marine
P.O. Box 56
Antioch

Carol's Harbor
Rt. 2, Box 340
Oakley

Collinsville Fishing Resort
Star Rt. 283, Box 125
Suisun

 # Antioch Area

Your Log Notes:

DELTA DIRECTORY

Fishing Supplies (Continued)

Inland Marine Service
Rt. 1, Box 524
Antioch

Lauritzen Yacht Harbor
Rt. 1, Box 515
Antioch

Lloyd's Holiday Harbor
Wilbur Ave.
Rt. 1, Box 553
Antioch

New Orwood Resort
Rt. 1, Box 88
Brentwood

Panfili's Bait Shop
Antioch

Pittsburg Yacht Harbor
5 Cutter St.
Pittsburg

Sam's Harbor
Rt. 2, Box 333
Oakley

Fuel

Bale's Bait Shop
Gasoline
Rt. 1, Box 500
Antioch

Big Break Resort
Gasoline
P.O. Box 171
Oakley

Carol's Harbor
Gasoline
Rt. 2, Box 340
Oakley

Collinsville Fishing Resort
Gasoline
Star Rt. 283, Box 125
Suisun

Delta Marine Center
Gasoline, Diesel
111 Fulton Shipyard Rd.
Antioch

Driftwood Marina
Gasoline, Diesel
P.O. Box 156
Antioch

Inland Marine Service
Gasoline, Diesel
Rt. 1, Box 524
Antioch

Lloyd's Holiday Harbor
Gasoline
Wilbur Ave.
Rt. 1, Box 553
Antioch

New Orwood Resort
Gasoline
Rt. 1, Box 88
Brentwood

Petri Yacht Harbor
Gasoline, Diesel
Rt. 1, Box 542
Antioch

Pittsburg Yacht Harbor
Gasoline, Diesel
5 Cutter St.
Pittsburg

Richard's Yacht Center
Gasoline, Diesel
404 Dutch Slough
Oakley

Sam's Harbor
Gasoline
Rt. 2, Box 333
Oakley

San Joaquin Yacht Harbor
Gasoline
Rt. 1, Box 566
Antioch

Sportsmen Yacht Club Inc.
Gasoline
Rt. 1, Box 565
Antioch

Tommy's Antioch Yacht Harbor
Gasoline
P.O. Box 756
Antioch

Launching Facilities

Antioch Public Launching Ramp
P.O. Box 369
Antioch

Big Break Resort
P.O. Box 171
Oakley

Carol's Harbor
Rt. 2, Box 340
Oakley

Collinsville Fishing Resort
Star Rt. 283, Box 125
Suisun

**Grizzly Island Wildlife Area
Boat Launching Ramp**
Box 368
Suisun City

Lauritzen Yacht Harbor
Rt. 1, Box 515
Antioch

New Orwood Resort
Rt. 1, Box 88
Brentwood

Pittsburg Yacht Harbor
5 Cutter St.
Pittsburg

Sam's Harbor
Rt. 2, Box 333
Oakley

Moorage

Big Break Resort
P.O. Box 171
Oakley

Cachalot Harbor
Rt. 2, Box 377
Oakley

Carol's Harbor
Rt. 2, Box 340
Oakley

Collinsville Fishing Resort
Star Rt. 283, Box 125
Suisun

Delta Marine Center
111 Fulton Shipyard Rd.
Antioch

Driftwood Marina
P.O. Box 156
Antioch

Jay's Harbor
Box 453
Antioch

Lauritzen Yacht Harbor
Rt. 1, Box 515
Antioch

Lloyd's Holiday Harbor
Wilbur Ave.
Rt. 1, Box 553
Antioch

New Orwood Resort
Rt. 1, Box 88
Brentwood

Petri Yacht Harbor
Rt. 1, Box 542
Antioch

Pittsburg Yacht Harbor
5 Cutter St.
Pittsburg

Rivers Harbor
Rt. 2, Box 450
Oakley

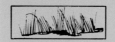 # Antioch Area

Your Log Notes:

DELTA DIRECTORY

155

Moorage (Continued)

Sam's Harbor
Rt. 2, Box 333
Oakley

San Joaquin Yacht Harbor
Rt. 1, Box 566
Antioch

Tommy's Antioch Yacht Harbor
P.O. Box 756
Antioch

Viking Harbor
Rt. 2, Box 470
Oakley

Rentals

Big Break Resort
Fishing Boats, Outboard Motors
P.O. Box 171
Oakley

Carol's Harbor
Fishing Boats, Outboard Motors
Rt. 2, Box 340
Oakley

Collinsville Fishing Resort
Fishing Boats
Star Rt. 283, Box 125
Suisun

Delta Marine Center
Fishing Boats
111 Fulton Shipyard Rd.
Antioch

Ferreira's Marine
Outboard Motors
Antioch

Jay's Harbor
Fishing Boats
Box 453
Antioch

Lauritzen Yacht Harbor
Houseboats
Rt. 1, Box 515
Antioch

New Orwood Resort
Fishing Boats, Houseboats, Outboard Motors
Rt. 1, Box 88
Brentwood

Richard's Yacht Center
Houseboats, Fishing Boats
404 Dutch Slough
Oakley

S&H Boatyard
Houseboats
Rt. 1, Box 514
Antioch

Sam's Harbor
Fishing Boats
Rt. 2, Box 333
Oakley

Tommy's Antioch Harbor
Fishing Boats, Outboard Motors
P.O. Box 756
Antioch

Repairs

Big Break Resort
Hull, Prop & Shaft
P.O. Box 171
Oakley

Bridgehead Dry Dock
Engine, Hull, Prop & Shaft
Rt. 1, Box 554
Antioch

Carol's Harbor
Engine, Hull, Prop & Shaft
Rt. 2, Box 340
Oakley

Delta Marine Center
Engine, Hull
111 Fulton Shipyard Rd.
Antioch

Driftwood Marina
Engine
P.O. Box 156
Antioch

Ferreira's Marine
Engine
Antioch

Inland Marine Service
Engine
Rt. 1, Box 524
Antioch

Lauritzen Yacht Harbor
Hull
Rt. 1, Box 515
Antioch

Lloyd's Holiday Harbor
Engine, Hull, Prop & Shaft
Wilbur Ave.
Rt. 1, Box 553
Antioch

Marvin's Prop Shop
Prop & Shaft
701 Fulton Shipyard Rd.
Antioch

New Orwood Resort
Engine, Hull, Prop & Shaft
Rt. 1, Box 88
Brentwood

Petri Yacht Harbor
Engine
Rt. 1, Box 542
Antioch

Pittsburg Yacht Harbor
Engine, Hull, Prop & Shaft
5 Cutter St.
Pittsburg

Seeno E. Ramey Boat Works
Hull, Prop & Shaft
142 Merrill Drive
Antioch

Richard's Yacht Center
Engine
404 Dutch Slough
Oakley

S&H Boatyard
Hull
Rt. 1, Box 514
Antioch

Tommy's Antioch Yacht Harbor
Engine
P.O. Box 756
Antioch

 **Antioch Area**

Your Log Notes:

Thomas A. Short takes Tasco IV *into the broader reaches of the San Joaquin near Antioch headed for San Francisco.*
The dress flags denote years of attendance at St. Francis YC's Tinsley Island conclave.

DELTA DIRECTORY

Bethel Island and Adjacent Areas

The Bethel Island area is located to the east of the Antioch region in the middle Delta. The area includes, in addition to the main island, Holland Tract, the northwest corner of Bacon Island, Quimby Island, most of Mandeville Island, the southern portions of Webb Tract and Bradford Island and half of Jersey Island. The major waterways are Franks Tract Lake, False River, the southern half of Fisherman's Cut, Taylor Slough, the last few miles of Dutch Slough, Sandmound Slough, Rock Slough, Holland Cut and a piece of the Old River.

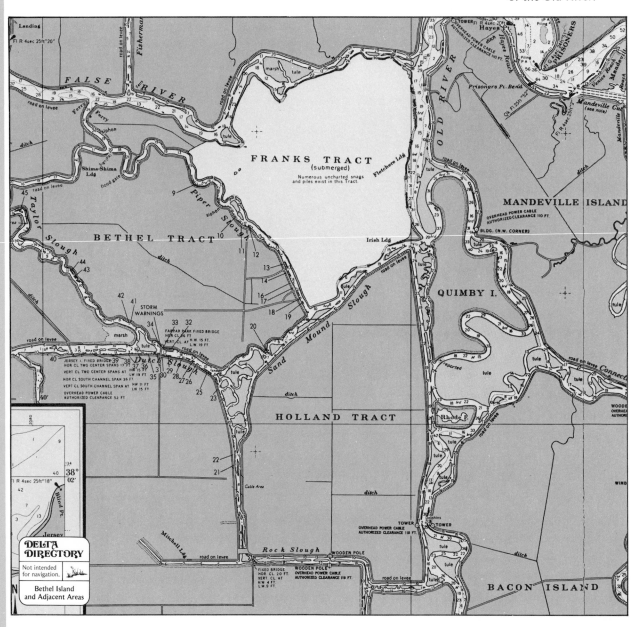

Camping

Bethel Harbor
3405 Harbor Rd.
Bethel Island

Greg's Motel & Harbor
3295 Wells Rd.
Box 114
Bethel Island

Frank's Fishing Resort
Bethel Island

Lin's Harbor
P.O. Box 622
Bethel Island

The Sugar Barge
520 Riverview Dr.
Bethel Island

Dining

The Boat House Lounge
Gateway Rd.
Bethel Island

Boyd's Harbor Resort
P.O. Box 68
Bethel Island

Chicken Shack Restaurant
Bethel Island

Delta Resort
P.O. Box 486
Bethel Island

Frank's Fishing Resort
Bethel Island

Gangplank Restaurant
P.O. Box 8
Bethel Island

Joseph's Harbor
P.O. Box 27
Bethel Island

Leisure Landing
P.O. Box 488
Bethel Island

Lin's Harbor
P.O. Box 622
Bethel Island

Marine Emporium
P.O. Box 637
Bethel Island

Rayette's Bar & Restaurant
Bethel Island

Russo's Marina & Cafe
P.O. Box 487
Bethel Island

The Sugar Barge
620 Riverview Dr.
Bethel Island

Bethel Island and Adjacent Areas

Your Log Notes:

DELTA DIRECTORY

Fishing Supplies

Bethel Harbor
3405 Harbor Rd.
Bethel Island

Frank's Fishing Resort
Bethel Island

George's Marine Center
P.O. Box 339
Bethel Island

Jonesy's Bait & Tackle
Box 39
Bethel Island

Lin's Harbor
P.O. Box 622
Bethel Island

Marine Emporium
P.O. Box 637
Bethel Island

Fuel

Anchor Marina
Gasoline
P.O. Box 56
Bethel Island

Beacon Harbor
Gasoline
P.O. Box 346
Bethel Island

Bethel Harbor
Gasoline
3405 Harbor Rd.
Bethel Island

The Boat House
Gasoline
Bethel Island

Bob's Marina
Gasoline
Bethel Island

Boyd's Harbor Resort
Gasoline
P.O. Box 68
Bethel Island

Carter's Deluxe Houseboats
Gasoline
P.O. Box 209
Bethel Island

Delta Cruz Houseboat Rentals Inc.
Gasoline, Diesel
P.O. Box 392
Bethel Island

Delta Resort
Gasoline
P.O. Box 486
Bethel Island

Frank's Fishing Resort
Gasoline
Bethel Island

General Sales & Service
Gasoline
No. 2 Bethel Rd.
Bethel Island

George's Marine Center
Gasoline
P.O. Box 339
Bethel Island

Island Marina
Gasoline
P.O. Box 334
Bethel Island

Leisure Landing
Gasoline, Diesel
P.O. Box 488
Bethel Island

Lin's Harbor
Gasoline
P.O. Box 622
Bethel Island

Remsburg Harbor
Gasoline
Bethel Island Rd. & Dutch Slough
Bethel Island

Russo's Marina & Cafe
Gasoline
P.O. Box 487
Bethel Island

Wharf Yacht Sales
Gasoline
Box 433
Bethel Island

Willow Park Marina
Gasoline, Diesel
P.O. Box 392
Bethel Island

Wood's Yacht Harbor
Gasoline
Box 426
Bethel Island

Launching Facilities

Beacon Harbor
P.O. Box 346
Bethel Island

Bethel Harbor
3405 Harbor Rd.
Bethel Island

Bethel Island Dry Dock
Bethel Island

Farrar Park Harbor
P.O. Box 522
Bethel Island

Frank's Fishing Resort
Bethel Island

George's Marine Center
P.O. Box 339
Bethel Island

Island Marina
P.O. Box 334
Bethel Island

Lin's Harbor
P.O. Box 622
Bethel Island

Marine Emporium
P.O. Box 637
Bethel Island

Remsburg Harbor
Bethel Island Rd. & Dutch Slough
Bethel Island

Russo's Marina & Cafe
P.O. Box 487
Bethel Island

Moorage

Anchor Marina
P.O. Box 56
Bethel Island

Beacon Harbor
P.O. Box 346
Bethel Island

The Boat House
Bethel Island

Bob's Marina
Bethel Island

Brown's Marina
P.O. Box 72
Bethel Island

Carter's Deluxe Houseboats
P.O. Box 209
Bethel Island

Farrar Park Harbor
P.O. Box 522
Bethel Island

Frank's Fishing Resort
Bethel Island

George's Marine Center
P.O. Box 339
Bethel Island

Greg's Motel & Harbor
3295 Wells Rd.
Box 114
Bethel Island

Hartman's Harbor
P.O. Box 116
Bethel Island

Island Marina
P.O. Box 334
Bethel Island

Jonesy's Bait & Tackle
Box 39
Bethel Island

Joseph's Harbor
P.O. Box 27
Bethel Island

Bethel Island and Adjacent Areas

Your Log Notes:

DELTA DIRECTORY

Moorage (Continued)

Leisure Landing
P.O. Box 488
Bethel Island

Lin's Harbor
P.O. Box 622
Bethel Island

Marine Emporium
P.O. Box 637
Bethel Island

Noler's Lakeview Harbor
P.O. Box 138
Bethel Island

Prince Harbor
Box 447
Bethel Island

Remsburg Harbor
Bethel Island Rd. & Dutch Slough
Bethel Island

Riskin's Marina
Bethel Island

Riverview Resort
6767 Riverview Dr., Box 21
Bethel Island

Russo's Marina & Cafe
P.O. Box 487
Bethel Island

Seven Bells Harbor
2620 Taylor Rd.
Bethel Island

The Sugar Barge
620 Riverview Dr.
Bethel Island

Willow Park Marina
P.O. Box 392
Bethel Island

Wood's Yacht Harbor
Box 426
Bethel Island

Rentals

Boyd's Harbor Resort
Fishing Boats, Outboard Motors
P.O. Box 68
Bethel Island

Carter's Deluxe Houseboats
Fishing Boats, Houseboats
P.O. Box 209
Bethel Island

Delta Cruz Houseboat Rentals Inc.
Houseboats
P.O. Box 392
Bethel Island

Delta Resort
Fishing Boats, Houseboats, Outboard Motors
P.O. Box 486
Bethel Island

Frank's Fishing Resort
Fishing Boats, Outboard Motors
Bethel Island

General Sales & Service
Fishing Boats, Houseboats, Outboard Motors
No. 2 Bethel Rd.
Bethel Island

George's Marine Center
Fishing Boats, Outboard Motors
P.O. Box 339
Bethel Island

Island Marina
Fishing Boats
P.O. Box 334
Bethel Island

Lin's Harbor
Fishing Boats
P.O. Box 622
Bethel Island

Marine Emporium
Fishing Boats, Outboard Motors
P.O. Box 637
Bethel Island

Russo's Marina & Cafe
Fishing Boats, Outboard Motors
P.O. Box 487
Bethel Island

The Sugar Barge
Fishing Boats
620 Riverview Dr.
Bethel Island

VIP Houseboat Rentals
Houseboats
3307 Wells Rd.
Bethel Island

Willow Park Marina
Houseboats
P.O. Box 392
Bethel Island

Wood's Yacht Harbor
Fishing Boats, Houseboats
Box 426
Bethel Island

Repairs

Bethel Island Dry Dock
Engine
Bethel Island

Carter's Deluxe Houseboats
Engine
P.O. Box 209
Bethel Island

Crosby Outboard Repair
Engine
Bethel Island

Delta Cruz Houseboat Rentals Inc.
Engine
P.O. Box 392
Bethel Island

Delta Resort
Engine
P.O. Box 486
Bethel Island

Diamond Yacht & Outboard Marina
Engine
P.O. Box 531
Bethel Island

Farrar Park Harbor
Engine, Hull, Prop & Shaft
P.O. Box 522
Bethel Island

Frank's Fishing Resort
Engine
Bethel Island

General Sales & Service
Engine
No. 2 Bethel Rd.
Bethel Island

George's Marine Center
Engine, Hull
P.O. Box 339
Bethel Island

Greg's Motel & Harbor
Engine
3295 Wells Rd., Box 114
Bethel Island

Island Marina
Engine
P.O. Box 334
Bethel Island

Island Marine Sales & Service
Engine
P.O. Box 334
Bethel Island

Joseph's Harbor
Engine
P.O. Box 27
Bethel Island

Marine Emporium
Hull, Prop & Shaft
P.O. Box 637
Bethel Island

Moody's Boat Prop Repair
Prop & Shaft
54 Bethel Island Rd.
Bethel Island

Noler's Lakeview Harbor
Engine
P.O. Box 138
Bethel Island

Walt Pierce Marine Service
Engine, Hull, Prop & Shaft
5614 Sandmound Blvd., P.O. Box B-H
Bethel Island

Willow Park Marina
Engine
P.O. Box 392
Bethel Island

Bethel Island and Adjacent Areas

Your Log Notes:

DELTA DIRECTORY

Rio Vista, Isleton and Terminous Area

The Rio Vista, Isleton and Terminous area straddles the middle and northern regions of the Delta. Its boundaries run from Webb Tract, Bradford Island and the tip of Sherman Island in the south, west across the Sacramento River to Rio Vista and then back across the river through the southern sections of Ryer and Grand islands, finally bisecting Andrus, Tyler and Staten islands. On the east, its borders cut through King Island and Empire Tract and skirt the city of Terminous.

The area contains long stretches of the San Joaquin and Sacramento rivers, the south and north forks of the Mokelumne River, Sycamore, Jackson, Sevenmile, Threemile, Potato, Little Potato, Whites, Steamboat and Hog sloughs and Fishermans Cut. These waterways enclose Bouldin, Venice, Twitchell and Brannan islands.

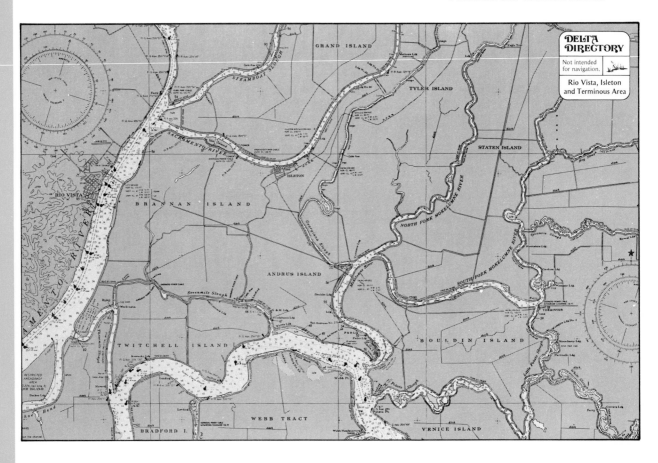

Camping

Brannan Island State Recreation Area
Star Rt., Box 75A
Rio Vista

Bruno's Boat Harbor
P.O. Box 638
Isleton

Eddo's Boat Harbor
Star Rt., Box 140A
Rio Vista

Greening's Ko-Ket Resort
Rt. 1, Box 15
Isleton

Happy Harbor & Trailer Park
Rt. 1, Box 64
Isleton

Hap's Bait & Sport Store
84 Main St.
Rio Vista

Korth's Pirates Lair Marina
Rt. 1, Box 63
Isleton

Lighthouse Resort
Rt. 1, Box 58
Isleton

Rancho Marina
Rt. 1, Box 57
Isleton

Dining

Bean Pot Cafe
Rio Vista

Bernie's
32 Main St.
Isleton

Bruno's Boat Harbor
P.O. Box 638
Isleton

Cliff House
Rt. 1, Box 77C
Isleton

Del Rio Hotel
Isleton

Delta Marina
100 Marina Dr.
Rio Vista

Ernie's
212 Second St.
Isleton

Fishing Resort
Rt. 1, Box 77C
Isleton

Foster's Big Horn *
143 Main St.
Rio Vista

Facilities not located on the water *

Rio Vista, Isleton and Terminous Area

Your Log Notes:

DELTA DIRECTORY

Dining (Continued)

Greening's Ko-Ket Resort
Rt. 1, Box 15
Isleton

Korth's Pirates Lair Marina
Rt. 1, Box 63
Isleton

Len's Fishing Resort
Sherman Island Blvd.
Isleton

Lighthouse Resort
Rt. 1, Box 58
Isleton

The Outrigger
Rio Vista

The Point Restaurant
120 Marina Dr.
Rio Vista

Rancho Marina
Rt. 1, Box 57
Isleton

Riverboat Restaurant
At Moore's Yacht Haven
Rt. 1, Box 61
Isleton

Sacramento Owens Yacht Sales
At B&W Boat Harbor
Box 52-B
Isleton

San Andreas Boat Harbor
Isleton

Spindrift Marina
Rt. 1, Box 67F
Isleton

Sycamore Park
Isleton

Van's Resort
Hwy. 160
Rio Vista

Vieria's Resort
Hwy. 160
Rio Vista

Fishing Supplies

B&W Resort
Rt. 1, Box 52
Isleton

Bean Pot Cafe
Rio Vista

Bruno's Boat Harbor
P.O. Box 638
Isleton

Cliff House
Rt. 1, Box 77C
Isleton

Delta Marina
100 Marina Dr.
Rio Vista

Eddo's Boat Harbor
Star Rt., Box 140A
Rio Vista

Fishing Resort
Rt. 1, Box 77C
Isleton

Greening's Ko-Ket Resort
Rt. 1, Box 15
Isleton

Happy Harbor & Trailer Park
Rt. 1, Box 64
Isleton

Hap's Bait & Sport Store
84 Main St.
Rio Vista

Lee's Bait
Isleton

Len's Fishing Resort
Sherman Island Blvd.
Isleton

Lighthouse Resort
Rt. 1, Box 58
Isleton

Monterey Bait & Tackle
154 N. Front St.
Rio Vista

The Outrigger
Rio Vista

Rancho Marina
Rt. 1, Box 57
Isleton

Sacramento Owens Yacht Sales
At B&W Boat Harbor
Box 52B
Isleton

San Andreas Boat Harbor
Isleton

Van's Resort
Hwy. 160
Rio Vista

Vieria's Resort
Hwy. 160
Rio Vista

Fuel

B&W Resort
Gasoline
Rt. 1, Box 52
Isleton

Bruno's Boat Harbor
Gasoline
P.O. Box 638
Isleton

Delta Marina
Gasoline
100 Marina Dr.
Rio Vista

Eddo's Boat Harbor
Gasoline
Star Rt., Box 140A
Rio Vista

Fishing Resort
Gasoline
Rt. 1, Box 77C
Isleton

Greening's Ko-Ket Resort
Gasoline
Rt. 1, Box 15
Isleton

Happy Harbor & Trailer Park
Gasoline
Rt. 1, Box 64
Isleton

Hap's Bait & Sport Store
Gasoline
84 Main St.
Rio Vista

Korth's Pirates Lair Marina
Gasoline
Rt. 1, Box 63
Isleton

Len's Fishing Resort
Gasoline
Sherman Island Blvd.
Isleton

Lighthouse Resort
Gasoline
Rt. 1, Box 58
Isleton

Moore's Riverboat Yacht Haven
Gasoline, Diesel
Rt. 1, Box 61
Isleton

The Outrigger
Gasoline
Rio Vista

Perry's Boat Harbor & Drydock Co.
Gasoline
P.O. Box 375
Isleton

Rancho Marina
Gasoline
Rt. 1, Box 57
Isleton

Sacramento Owens Yacht Sales
Gasoline
At B&W Boat Harbor
Box 52B
Isleton

San Andreas Boat Harbor
Gasoline
Isleton

Rio Vista, Isleton and Terminous Area

Your Log Notes:

DELTA DIRECTORY

Fuel (Continued)

Spindrift Marina
Gasoline
Rt. 1, Box 67F
Isleton

Sycamore Park
Gasoline
Isleton

Van's Resort
Gasoline
Hwy. 160
Rio Vista

Vieria's Resort
Gasoline
Hwy. 106
Rio Vista

Willow Berm Marina
Gasoline, Diesel
Rt. 1, Box 60
Isleton

Launching Facilities

B&W Resort
Rt. 1, Box 52
Isleton

Brannan Island State Recreation Area
Star Rt., Box 75A
Rio Vista

Del Rio Hotel
Isleton

Delta Marina
100 Marina Dr.
Rio Vista

Delta Marine Service
P.O. Box 362
Rio Vista

Greening's Ko-Ket Resort
Rt. 1, Box 15
Isleton

Hap's Bait & Sport Store
84 Main St.
Rio Vista

Korth's Pirates Lair Marina
Rt. 1, Box 63
Isleton

Lighthouse Resort
Rt. 1, Box 58
Isleton

Rancho Marina
Rt. 1, Box 57
Isleton

Rio Vista Public Launching Ramp
Main & Front Sts.
Rio Vista

Sacramento Owens Yacht Sales
At B&W Boat Harbor
Box 52B
Isleton

San Andreas Boat Harbor
Isleton

Sycamore Park
Isleton

Vieria's Resort
Hwy. 160
Rio Vista

Moorage

Bruno's Boat Harbor
P.O. Box 638
Isleton

Cliff House
Rt. 1, Box 77C
Isleton

Delta Marina
100 Marina Dr.
Rio Vista

Eddo's Boat Harbor
Star Rt., Box 140A
Rio Vista

Greening's Ko-Ket Resort
Rt. 1, Box 15
Isleton

Happy Harbor & Trailer Park
Rt. 1, Box 64
Isleton

Hap's Bait & Sport Store
84 Main St.
Rio Vista

Holiday Harbor
Isleton

Korth's Pirates Lair Marina
Rt. 1, Box 63
Isleton

Lighthouse Resort
Rt. 1, Box 58
Isleton

Moore's Riverboat Yacht Haven
Rt. 1, Box 61
Isleton

Perry's Boat Harbor & Drydock Co.
P.O. Box 375
Isleton

Rancho Marina
Rt. 1, Box 57
Isleton

Sacramento Owens Yacht Sales
At B&W Boat Harbor
Box 52B
Isleton

San Andreas Boat Harbor
Isleton

Spindrift Marina
Rt. 1, Box 67F
Isleton

Sycamore Park
Isleton

Vieria's Resort
Hwy. 160
Rio Vista

Willow Berm Marina
Rt. 1, Box 60
Isleton

Rentals

B&W Resort
Fishing Boats, Houseboats, Outboard Motors
Rt. 1, Box 52
Isleton

Bruno's Boat Harbor
Fishing Boats, Houseboats, Outboard Motors
P.O. Box 638
Isleton

Cliff House
Fishing Boats, Outboard Motors
Rt. 1, Box 77C
Isleton

Eddo's Boat Harbor
Fishing Boats, Houseboats, Outboard Motors
Star Rt., Box 140A
Rio Vista

Fishing Resort
Fishing Boats, Outboard Motors
Rt. 1, Box 77C
Isleton

Happy Harbor & Trailer Park
Fishing Boats
Rt. 1, Box 64
Isleton

Hap's Bait & Sport Store
Fishing Boats
84 Main St.
Rio Vista

Korth's Pirates Lair Marina
Fishing Boats, Outboard Motors
Rt. 1, Box 63
Isleton

Len's Fishing Resort
Fishing Boats
Sherman Island Blvd.
Isleton

Lighthouse Resort
Fishing Boats
Rt. 1, Box 57
Isleton

The Outrigger
Fishing Boats, Outboard Motors
Rio Vista

Rio Vista, Isleton and Terminous Area

Your Log Notes:

DELTA DIRECTORY

Rentals (Continued)

Rancho Marina
Fishing Boats
Rt. 1, Box 57
Isleton

Sacramento Owens Yacht Sales
Fishing Boats, Houseboats
At B&W Boat Harbor
Box 52B
Isleton

San Andreas Boat Harbor
Fishing Boats
Isleton

Sycamore Park
Fishing Boats
Isleton

Van's Resort
Fishing Boats
Hwy. 160
Rio Vista

Vieria's Resort
Fishing Boats
Hwy. 160
Rio Vista

Repairs

Delta Marina
Engine, Hull, Prop & Shaft
100 Marina Dr.
Rio Vista

Delta Marine Service
Engine, Hull, Prop & Shaft
P.O. Box 362
Rio Vista

Happy Harbor & Trailer Park
Engine, Prop & Shaft
Rt. 1, Box 64
Isleton

Korth's Pirates Lair Marina
Engine
Rt. 1, Box 63
Isleton

Moore's Riverboat Yacht Haven
Engine, Hull, Prop & Shaft
Rt. 1, Box 61
Isleton

Perry's Boat Harbor & Drydock Co.
Engine, Hull, Prop & Shaft
P.O. Box 375
Isleton

Vieria's Resort
Engine
Hwy. 160
Rio Vista

Rio Vista, Isleton and Terminous Area

Your Log Notes:

Aerial view of the Delta Marina and the Point Restaurant at Rio Vista. The city center and old-time waterfront are upstream to the right.

Stockton and South Delta Area

This is the largest area in the Delta region. Its boundaries describe an arc with the city of Stockton at the hub. The arc extends from Cohn Tract in the north through most of King Island, the southern portions of Empire Tract and Mandeville Island, the bulk of Bacon Island, the city of Byron, Veale and Clifton Court tracts over to Tracy, Lathrop, Manteca and adjacent areas in the south and southeast. Numerous waterways cut across the area including the San Joaquin, Middle, Old, and Calaveras rivers; Whiskey, Connection, Disappointment, Salmon, Tom Paine and Trapper sloughs; the Victoria, Woodward and Grant Line canals and Turner Cut.

Major land areas in the Stockton-middle Delta territory are Rindge, Shima, McDonald, Henning and Elmwood tracts, Medford, Mildred and lower Roberts islands and downtown Stockton. The south Delta encompasses Palm, Orwood, Lower Jones, Upper Jones and Fabian tracts; upper Roberts, Woodward, Victoria and Union islands; French Camp and the cities of Holt, Banta, Bethany and Turner.

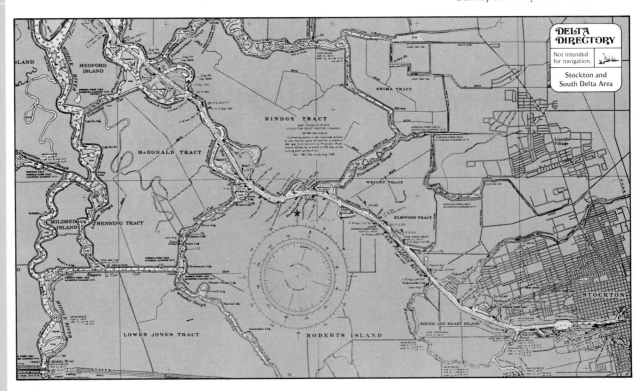

Camping

D&Y River Club
1691 W. Frewert Rd.
Lathrop

The Islander Marina & Trailer Park *
20801 S. Woodward
Manteca

Lost Isle Marina
Stockton

Mossdale Park
J. 10 W. Hwy. 50
Lathrop

Tiki Lagun Resort Marina
12988 W. McDonald Rd.
Stockton

Tony's Boat Harbor
14320 W. Grimes Rd.
Tracy

Turner Cut Resort
12888 W. Neugebauer Rd.
Stockton

Uncle Bobbie's Marine Sales & Service
11520 W. 8 Mile Rd.
Stockton

Wetherbee Lake & Trailer Park *
703 Williamson Rd.
Manteca

Windmill Cove
3630 Holt Rd.
Stockton

Dining

Del's Boat Harbor
Box 20
Tracy

Ehrich's Fishing Resort
10941 W. Neugebauer Rd.
Stockton

Heinbockle Harbor
11714 W. Finck Rd.
Tracy

Herman & Helen's Resort
Venice Island Ferry
Stockton

Holiday Inn of Stockton
221 N. Center
Stockton

The Islander Marina & Trailer Park *
20801 S. Woodward Ave.
Manteca

King Island Resort Inc.
11530 W. 8 Mile Rd.
Stockton

Facilities not located on the water *

 # Stockton and South Delta Area

Your Log Notes:

DELTA DIRECTORY

173

Dining (Continued)

Ladd's Stockton Marina
P.O. Box 1385
Stockton

Lost Isle Marina
Stockton

Middle River Inn
17700 Bacon Island Rd.
General Delivery
Holt

Paradise Point
8095 Rio Blanco Rd.
Stockton

Tiki Lagun Resort Marina
12988 W. McDonald Rd.
Stockton

Tracy Oasis Marina
12450 W. Grimes Rd.
Tracy

Turner Cut Resort
12888 W. Neugebauer Rd.
Stockton

Uncle Tom's Cabin
Holt

Union Point Fishing Resort
P.O. Box 177
Holt

Uptown Yacht Harbor
200 W. Channel St.
Stockton

Wetherbee Lake & Trailer Park *
703 Williamson Rd.
Manteca

Whiskey Slough Harbor
P.O. Box 107
Holt

Windmill Cove
3630 Holt Rd.
Stockton

Fishing Supplies

Alex Boat Harbor
Byron

Ben's Place
J. 73 Stewart Rd.
Lathrop

D&Y River Club
1691 W. Frewert Rd.
Lathrop

Del's Boat Harbor
Box 20
Tracy

Ehrich's Fishing Resort
19041 W. Neugebauer Rd.
Stockton

Heinbockle Harbor
11714 W. Finck Rd.
Tracy

Herman & Helen's Resort
Venice Island Ferry
Stockton

The Islander Marina & Trailer Park *
20801 S. Woodward Ave.
Manteca

King Island Resort Inc.
11530 W. 8 Mile Rd.
Stockton

Lost Isle Marina
Stockton

Louis Park Fore 'n Aft
3303 Mt. Diablo Ave.
Stockton

Chet Moylie's Boats
c/o Pop's Boats, Via Mail Boat
Bacon Island
Stockton

Paradise Point
8095 Rio Blanco Rd.
Stockton

Tony's Boat Harbor
14320 W. Grimes Rd.
Tracy

Tracy Oasis Marina
12450 W. Grimes Rd.
Tracy

Turner Cut Resort
12888 W. Neugebauer Rd.
Stockton

Uncle Bobbie's Marine Sales & Service
11520 W. 8 Mile Rd.
Stockton

Uncle Tom's Cabin
Holt

Union Point Fishing Resort
P.O. Box 177
Holt

Wetherbee Lake & Trailer Park *
703 Williamson Rd.
Manteca

Whiskey Slough Harbor
P.O. Box 107
Holt

Fuel

Alex Boat Harbor
Gasoline
Byron

Calcagno's Yacht Sales
Gasoline
200 W. Miner Ave.
Stockton

174

D&Y River Club
Gasoline
1691 W. Frewert Rd.
Lathrop

Del's Boat Harbor
Gasoline
Box 20
Tracy

Ehrich's Fishing Resort
Gasoline
10941 W. Neugebauer Rd.
Stockton

Habeeb Boat House
Gasoline
120 Steamboat Levee
Stockton

Heinbockle Harbor
Gasoline
11714 W. Finck Rd.
Tracy

Herman & Helen's Resort
Gasoline, Diesel
Venice Island Ferry
Stockton

Hoffman Anchorage at Buckley Cove
Gasoline, Diesel
4950 W. Brookside Rd.
Stockton

The Islander Marina & Trailer Park *
Gasoline
20801 S. Woodward Ave.
Manteca

King Island Resort, Inc.
Gasoline
11530 W. 8 Mile Rd.
Stockton

Lost Isle Marina
Gasoline, Diesel
Stockton

Louis Park Fore 'n Aft
Gasoline, Diesel
3303 Mt. Diablo Ave.
Stockton

New Marina Yacht Harbor
Gasoline
345 N. Center
Stockton

Paradise Point
Gasoline
8095 Rio Blanco Rd.
Stockton

Pop's Boats
Gasoline
Bacon Island
Stockton

Facilities not located on the water *

Stockton and South Delta Area

Your Log Notes:

DELTA DIRECTORY

Fuel (Continued)

Tiki Lagun Resort Marina
Gasoline
12988 W. McDonald Rd.
Stockton

Tony's Boat Harbor
Gasoline
14320 W. Grimes Rd.
Tracy

Tracy Oasis Marina
Gasoline
12450 W. Grimes Rd.
Tracy

Turner Cut Resort
Gasoline, Diesel
12888 W. Neugebauer Rd.
Stockton

Uncle Bobbie's Marine Sales & Service
Gasoline
11520 W. 8 Mile Rd.
Stockton

Uncle Tom's Cabin
Gasoline
Holt

Union Point Fishing Resort
Gasoline
P.O. Box 177
Holt

Uptown Yacht Harbor
Gasoline
200 W. Channel St.
Stockton

Wetherbee Lake & Trailer Park *
Gasoline
703 Williamson Rd.
Manteca

Whiskey Slough Harbor
Gasoline
P.O. Box 107
Holt

Windmill Cove
Gasoline
3630 Holt Rd.
Stockton

Launching Facilities

D&Y River Club
1691 W. Frewert Rd.
Lathrop

Del's Boat Harbor
Box 20
Tracy

Heinbockle Harbor
11714 W. Finck Rd.
Tracy

Hoffman Anchorage at Buckley Cove
4950 W. Brookside Rd.
Stockton

The Islander Marina & Trailer Park *
20801 S. Woodward Ave.
Manteca

Ladd's Stockton Marina
P.O. Box 1385
Stockton

Louis Park Fore 'n Aft
3303 Mt. Diablo Ave.
Stockton

Mossdale Park
J. 10 W. Hwy. 50
Lathrop

New Marina Yacht Harbor
345 N. Center
Stockton

Paradise Point
8095 Rio Blanco Rd.
Stockton

Tiki Lagun Resort Marina
12988 W. McDonald Rd.
Stockton

Tony's Boat Harbor
14320 W. Grimes Rd.
Tracy

Tracy Oasis Marina
12450 W. Grimes Rd.
Tracy

Uncle Bobbie's Marine Sales & Service
11520 W. 8 Mile Rd.
Stockton

Wetherbee Lake & Trailer Park *
703 Williamson Rd.
Manteca

Windmill Cove
3630 Holt Rd.
Stockton

Moorage

Alex Boat Harbor
Byron

Delta Yacht Harbor
200 W. Miner Ave.
Stockton

Ehrich's Fishing Resort
10941 W. Neugebauer Rd.
Stockton

Habeeb Boat House
120 Steamboat Levee
Stockton

Hoffman Anchorage at Buckley Cove
4950 W. Brookside Rd.
Stockton

The Islander Marina & Trailer Park *
20801 S. Woodward Ave.
Manteca

Ladd's Stockton Marina
P.O. Box 1385
Stockton

Lincoln Village West Marina   *
3634 Harpers Ferry Dr.
Stockton

Lost Isle Marina
Stockton

New Marina Yacht Harbor
345 N. Center
Stockton

Paradise Point
8095 Rio Blanco Rd.
Stockton

Pop's Boats
Bacon Island
Stockton

Tiki Lagun Resort Marina
12988 W. McDonald Rd.
Stockton

Tony's Boat Harbor
14320 W. Grimes Rd.
Tracy

Tracy Oasis Marina
12450 W. Grimes Rd.
Tracy

Turner Cut Resort
12888 W. Neugebauer Rd.
Stockton

Uncle Bobbie's Marine Sales & Service
11520 W. 8 Mile Rd.
Stockton

Uptown Yacht Harbor
200 W. Channel St.
Stockton

Wetherbee Lake & Trailer Park   *
703 Williamson Rd.
Manteca

Whiskey Slough Harbor
P.O. Box 107
Holt

Rentals

Alex Boat Harbor
Fishing Boats, Outboard Motors
Byron

Ben's Place
Fishing Boats
J. 73 Stewart Rd.
Lathrop

Calcagno's Yacht Sales
Houseboats
200 W. Miner Ave.
Stockton

Facilities not located on the water   *

 # Stockton and South Delta Area

Your Log Notes:

Rentals (Continued)

Del's Boat Harbor
Fishing Boats, Outboard Motors
Box 20
Tracy

Ehrich's Fishing Resort
Fishing Boats, Outboard Motors
10941 W. Neugebauer Rd.
Stockton

Habeeb Boat House
Houseboats, Fishing Boats
120 Steamboat Levee
Stockton

Heinbockle Harbor
Outboard Motors
11714 W. Finck Rd.
Tracy

Herman & Helen's Resort
Fishing Boats, Outboard Motors
Venice Island Ferry
Stockton

Holiday Flotels — Delta *
Houseboats
P.O. Box 8771
Stockton

The Islander Marina & Trailer Park *
Fishing Boats, Outboard Motors
20801 S. Woodward Ave.
Manteca

King Island Resort Inc.
Fishing Boats, Outboard Motors
11530 W. 8 Mile Rd.
Stockton

Ladd's Stockton Marina
Houseboats
P.O. Box 1385
Stockton

Lost Isle Marina
Fishing Boats
Stockton

Louis Park Fore 'n Aft
Fishing Boats, Outboard Motors
3303 Mt. Diablo Ave.
Stockton

Magic Holiday Flotels Inc.
Houseboats
8020 W. Atherton Rd.
Stockton

Chet Moylie's Boats
Fishing Boats, Outboard Motors
c/o Pop's Boats
Bacon Island
Stockton

New Marina Yacht Harbor
Fishing Boats, Houseboats, Outboard Motors
345 W. Center
Stockton

Paradise Point
Fishing Boats, Houseboats
8095 Rio Blanco Rd.
Stockton

Pop's Boats
Fishing Boats, Outboard Motors
Bacon Island
Stockton

Stockton Luxury Houseboat Rentals
Houseboats
200 W. Channel St.
Stockton

Tiki Lagun Resort Marina
Houseboats
12988 W. McDonald Rd.
Stockton

Tony's Boat Harbor
Fishing Boats
14320 W. Grimes Rd.
Tracy

Turner Cut Resort
Fishing Boats, Outboard Motors
12888 W. Neugebauer Rd.
Stockton

Uncle Bobbie's Marine Sales & Service
Fishing Boats, Houseboats, Outboard Motors
11520 W. 8 Mile Rd.
Stockton

Uncle Tom's Cabin
Fishing Boats
Holt

Union Point Fishing Resort
Fishing Boats
P.O. Box 177
Holt

Uptown Yacht Harbor
Fishing Boats
200 W. Channel St.
Stockton

Wetherbee Lake & Trailer Park *
Fishing Boats
703 Williamson Rd.
Manteca

Whiskey Slough Harbor
Fishing Boats, Houseboats, Outboard Motors
P.O. Box 107
Holt

Windmill Cove
Houseboats
3630 Holt Rd.
Stockton

Repairs

Besotes Bros. Boats *
Hull
519 N. Sierra Nevada St.
Stockton

Calcagno's Yacht Sales
Engine, Hull, Prop & Shaft
200 W. Miner Ave.
Stockton

Colberg Inc.
Hull, Prop & Shaft
Stockton & Lindsay Sts.
Stockton

Hoffman Anchorage at Buckley Cove
Engine
4950 W. Brookside Rd.
Stockton

The Islander Marina & Trailer Park   *
Engine
20801 S. Woodward Ave.
Manteca

Ladd's Stockton Marina
Hull, Prop & Shaft
P.O. Box 1385
Stockton

New Marina Yacht Harbor
Engine, Hull, Prop & Shaft
345 N. Center
Stockton

Stephens Marine Inc.
Engine, Hull, Prop & Shaft
Box 670
Stockton

Stockton Marine   *
Engine
1748 W. Fremont
Stockton

Tony's Boat Harbor
Engine, Hull
14320 W. Grimes Rd.
Tracy

Uncle Bobbie's Marine Sales & Service
Engine, Hull
11520 W. 8 Mile Rd.
Stockton

Uptown Yacht Harbor
Engine
200 W. Channel St.
Stockton

Valley Marine
Engine, Prop & Shaft
2458 E. Waterloo Rd.
Stockton

Facilities not located on the water   *

 # Stockton and South Delta Area

Your Log Notes:

DELTA DIRECTORY

Walnut Grove-Courtland Area

The cities of Walnut Grove and Courtland on the Sacramento River lie at the center of this upper Delta area which extends as far north as five miles above Courtland and as far south as Lodi. The major water routes are the Sacramento, Mokelumne and Cosumnes rivers; Snodgrass, Steamboat, Haas, Lindsey, Cache, Georgiana, Beaver, Lost, Sutter, Miner and Prospect sloughs; the Sacramento Deep Water Channel, Liberty and Hastings Cuts, which serve as the westernmost boundary of the area. Important land areas are Ryer, Grand, Liberty and Sutter islands and the upper halves of Andrus, Tyler and Staten islands.

The smaller towns of Ryde and Locke are located on the Sacramento River and Lodi is situated at the foot of the Mokelumne River.

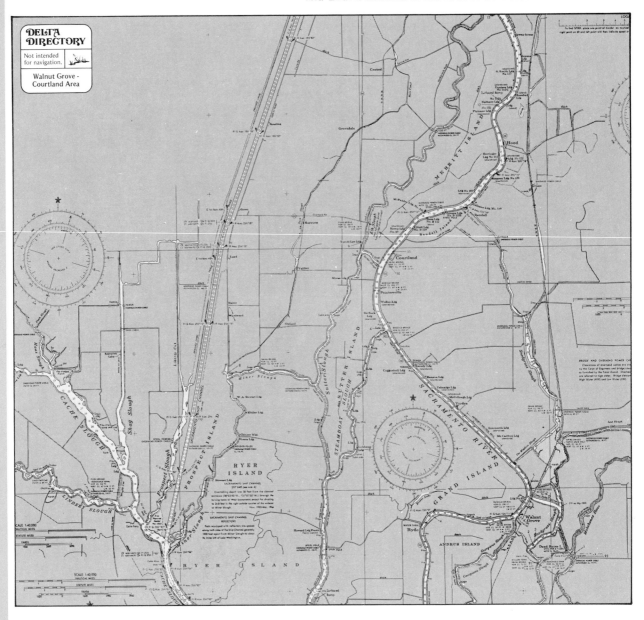

Camping

Hidden Harbor Resort
Rt. 1, Box 76
Walnut Grove

Snug Harbor Resort
Rt. 1, Box 70
Walnut Grove

New Hope Landing & Trailer Park
Box 417
Thornton

Tower Park Marina Resort
14300 N. Potatoe Rd.
Lodi

Dining

Al's Place
Locke

Bayport on the Delta
14711 Terminous Dr.
Lodi

Courtland Docks
Box 296
Courtland

Giusti's Resort
Walnut Grove

Hidden Harbor Resort
Rt. 1, Box 76
Walnut Grove

Morgan's Landing
Courtland

Sid's Holiday Harbor
Rt. 1, Box 44G
Walnut Grove

The Steamboater
Steamboat Slough
Walnut Grove

Tower Park Marina Resort
14300 N. Potatoe Rd.
Lodi

Walnut Grove Marina
P.O. Box 231
Walnut Grove

Wimpy's New Hope Cafe
P.O. Box 186
Thornton

Fishing Supplies

Bayport on the Delta
14711 Terminous Dr.
Lodi

Courtland Docks
Box 296
Courtland

Grindstone Joe's Association
13551 Little Potatoe Rd.
Lodi

Walnut Grove - Courtland Area

Your Log Notes:

DELTA DIRECTORY

Fishing Supplies (Continued)

Morgan's Landing
Courtland

New Hope Landing & Trailer Park
Box 417
Thornton

Sid's Holiday Harbor
Rt. 1, Box 44G
Walnut Grove

Tower Park Marina Resort
14300 N. Potatoe Rd.
Lodi

Walnut Grove Marina
P.O. Box 231
Walnut Grove

Wimpy's New Hope Marina
P.O. Box 186
Thornton

Fuel

Bayport on the Delta
Gasoline
14711 Terminous Dr.
Lodi

The Boat House
Gasoline
P.O. Box 798
Walnut Grove

Courtland Docks
Gasoline
Box 296
Courtland

Giusti's Resort
Gasoline
Walnut Grove

Hidden Harbor Resort
Gasoline
Rt. 1, Box 76
Walnut Grove

International Houseboat & Recreation Inc.
Gasoline
Box 342
Walnut Grove

Morgan's Landing
Gasoline
Courtland

New Hope Landing & Trailer Park
Gasoline
Box 417
Thornton

Sid's Holiday Harbor
Gasoline
Rt. 1, Box 44G
Walnut Grove

Snug Harbor Resort
Gasoline
Rt. 1, Box 70
Walnut Grove

Tower Park Marina Resort
Gasoline
14300 N. Potatoe Rd.
Lodi

Walnut Grove Marina
Gasoline
P.O. Box 231
Walnut Grove

Wimpy's New Hope Marina
Gasoline
P.O. Box 186
Thornton

Launching Facilities

Bayport on the Delta
14711 Terminous Dr.
Lodi

The Boat House
P.O. Box 798
Walnut Grove

Courtland Docks
Box 296
Courtland

Morgan's Landing
Courtland

New Hope Landing & Trailer Park
Box 417
Thornton

Sid's Holiday Harbor
Rt. 1, Box 44G
Walnut Grove

Snug Harbor Resort
Rt. 1, Box 70
Walnut Grove

Tower Park Marina Resort
14300 N. Potatoe Rd.
Lodi

Wimpy's New Hope Marina
P.O. Box 186
Thornton

Moorage

Bayport on the Delta
14711 Terminous Dr.
Lodi

Courtland Docks
Box 296
Courtland

Grindstone Joe's Association
13551 Little Potatoe Rd.
Lodi

Hidden Harbor Resort
Rt. 1, Box 76
Walnut Grove

New Hope Landing & Trailer Park
Box 417
Thornton

Snug Harbor Resort
Rt. 1, Box 70
Walnut Grove

Walnut Grove Marina
P.O. Box 231
Walnut Grove

Wimpy's New Hope Marina
P.O. Box 186
Thornton

Rentals

Bayport on the Delta
Fishing Boats, Outboard Motors
14711 Terminous Dr.
Lodi

Courtland Docks
Fishing Boats, Outboard Motors
Box 296
Courtland

Hidden Harbor Resort
Fishing Boats, Houseboats, Outboard Motors
Rt. 1, Box 76
Walnut Grove

International Houseboat & Recreation Inc.
Fishing Boats, Houseboats
Box 342
Walnut Grove

Morgan's Landing
Fishing Boats
Courtland

New Hope Landing & Trailer Park
Fishing Boats, Outboard Motors
Box 417
Thornton

Tower Park Marina Resort
Fishing Boats, Houseboats, Outboard Motors
14300 N. Potatoe Rd.
Lodi

Repairs

The Boat House
Engine, Hull
P.O. Box 798
Walnut Grove

Giusti's Resort
Engine
Walnut Grove

International Houseboat & Recreation Inc.
Engine, Hull
Box 342
Walnut Grove

New Hope Landing & Trailer Park
Engine
Box 417
Thornton

Wimpy's New Hope Marina
Engine, Hull, Prop & Shaft
P.O. Box 186
Thornton

Walnut Grove–Courtland Area

Your Log Notes:

DELTA DIRECTORY

Sacramento-Clarksburg Area

This northernmost region of the upper Delta extends north from the town of Hood, which is about halfway between Courtland and Clarksburg on the Sacramento River, to Marysville and Colusa and west to include Woodland. Most of the boating activity in the area, however, is centered on the stretch of the Sacramento River from Clarksburg and Freeport to the city of Sacramento itself.

Elk Slough parallels the Sacramento from Courtland to Clarksburg to form Merritt Island. Winchester Lake is located just a few miles north of the junction of the two rivers.

Major towns situated along the river include Freeport, Riverside, Sutterville, Bryte and Broderick which lies just south of the junction of the Sacramento and American rivers.

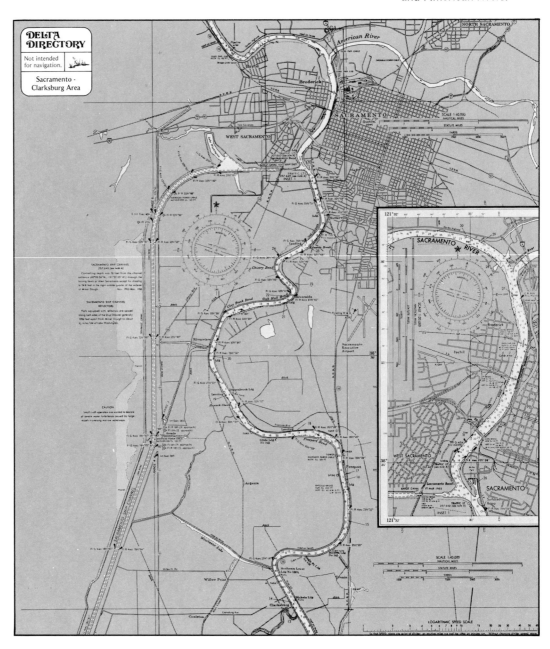

Camping

Cruise 'n Tarry Marina *
Rt. 1, Box 1890
Colusa

Dining

Alamar Landing
5999 Garden Hwy.
Sacramento

B&B Harbor
1361 Garden Highway
Sacramento

Clarksburg Landing
P.O. Box 127
Clarksburg

Cruise 'n Tarry Marina *
Rt. 1, Box 1890
Colusa

Freeport Marina Inc.
8250 Freeport Blvd.
Freeport

Stan's Freeport Baitshop & Marina
8250 Freeport Blvd.
Freeport

Tower Bridge Marina
P.O. Box 703
W. Sacramento

Village Marina
Rt. 3, Box 385
Sacramento

Fishing Supplies

Alamar Landing
5999 Garden Hwy.
Sacramento

B&B Harbor
1361 Garden Highway
Sacramento

Bud's Bait & Tackle
Freeport Blvd.
Sacramento

Clarksburg Landing
P.O. Box 127
Clarksburg

Cliff's Place
8651 River Rd.
Sacramento

Cruise 'n Tarry Marina *
Rt. 1, Box 1890
Colusa

Facilities not located on the water *

 # Sacramento-Clarksburg Area

Your Log Notes:

DELTA DIRECTORY

Fishing Supplies (Continued)

Dock Holiday
8140 Freeport Blvd.
Sacramento

Freeport Marina Inc.
8250 Freeport Blvd.
Freeport

Light 29 Marina
7948 Pocket Rd.
Sacramento

Riverside Marina
5804 Riverside Blvd.
Sacramento

Romeo's Bait Shop
8121 Freeport Blvd.
Sacramento

Stan's Freeport Baitshop & Marina
8250 Freeport Blvd.
Freeport

Tower Bridge Marina
P.O. Box 703
W. Sacramento

Fuel

Alamar Landing
Gasoline, Diesel
5999 Garden Hwy.
Sacramento

B&B Harbor
Gasoline
1361 Garden Highway
Sacramento

Cliff's Place
Gasoline
8651 River Rd.
Sacramento

Cruise 'n Tarry Marina *
Gasoline
Rt. 1, Box 1890
Colusa

Freeport Marina Inc.
Gasoline, Diesel
8250 Freeport Blvd.
Freeport

Mal's Garcia Bend Landing
Gasoline
South River Rd.
West Sacramento

Miller Park Boat Harbor
Gasoline
P.O. Box 1146
Sacramento

Riverside Marina
Gasoline
5804 Riverside Blvd.
Sacramento

Stan's Freeport Baitshop & Marina
Gasoline, Diesel
8250 Freeport Blvd.
Freeport

Tower Bridge Marina
Gasoline
P.O. Box 703
W. Sacramento

Village Marina
Gasoline
Rt. 3, Box 385
Sacramento

Launching Facilities

Austin's Boat Landing
South River Rd.
Sacramento

Clarksburg Marina
Box 67
Clarksburg

Cliff's Place
8651 River Rd.
Sacramento

Cruise 'n Tarry Marina *
Rt. 1, Box 1890
Colusa

Discovery Park
Sacramento

Erv's Boat Landing
Riverside Blvd.
Sacramento

Freeport Marina Inc.
8250 Freeport Blvd.
Freeport

Mal's Garcia Bend Landing
South River Rd.
West Sacramento

Miller Park Boat Harbor
P.O. Box 1146
Sacramento

Riverside Marina
5804 Riverside Blvd.
Sacramento

Tower Bridge Marina
P.O. Box 703
W. Sacramento

Village Marina
Rt. 3, Box 385
Sacramento

Moorage

Alamar Landing
5999 Garden Hwy.
Sacramento

Austin's Boat Landing
South River Rd.
Sacramento

B&B Harbor
1361 Garden Highway
Sacramento

Clarksburg Landing
P.O. Box 127
Clarksburg

Clarksburg Marina
Box 67
Clarksburg

Cliff's Place
8651 River Rd.
Sacramento

Cruise 'n Tarry Marina *
Rt. 1, Box 1890
Colusa

Elkhorn Marina
Levy Rd.
Broderick

Erv's Boat Landing
Riverside Blvd.
Sacramento

Freeport Marina Inc.
8250 Freeport Blvd.
Freeport

Gardner's Landing
Clarksburg

Light 29 Marina
7948 Pocket Rd.
Sacramento

Loris Bros. Marina
4350 Riverside Blvd.
Sacramento

Mal's Garcia Bend Landing
South River Rd.
West Sacramento

Miller Park Boat Harbor
P.O. Box 1146
Sacramento

Riverside Marina
5804 Riverside Blvd.
Sacramento

Tower Bridge Marina
P.O. Box 703
W. Sacramento

Tye-A-Lee Docks
1619 Carnelian Ct.
Woodland

Village Marina
Rt. 3, Box 385
Sacramento

Facilities not located on the water *

 # Sacramento-Clarksburg Area

Your Log Notes:

DELTA DIRECTORY

Rentals

Alamar Landing
Fishing Boats, Houseboats, Outboard Motors
5999 Garden Hwy.
Sacramento

Clarksburg Landing
Fishing Boats, Outboard Motors
P.O. Box 127
Clarksburg

Cliff's Place
Fishing Boats
8651 River Rd.
Sacramento

Cruise 'n Tarry Marina *
Fishing Boats, Outboard Motors
Rt. 1, Box 1890
Colusa

Dock Holiday
Fishing Boats
8140 Freeport Blvd.
Sacramento

Freeport Marina Inc.
Fishing Boats, Outboard Motors
8250 Freeport Blvd.
Freeport

Light 29 Marina
Fishing Boats
7948 Pocket Rd.
Sacramento

Mal's Garcia Bend Landing
Fishing Boats, Outboard Motors
South River Rd.
West Sacramento

Riverside Marina
Fishing Boats
5804 Riverside Blvd.
Sacramento

Tower Bridge Marina
Houseboats
P.O. Box 703
West Sacramento

Repairs

Alamar Landing
Engine, Prop & Shaft
5999 Garden Hwy.
Sacramento

Capitol Marine Inc. *
Engine, Hull, Prop & Shaft
4720 Auburn Blvd.
Sacramento

Jeffries Motors *
Engine
941 N. Beale Rd.
Marysville

Miller Park Boat Harbor
Engine, Hull, Prop & Shaft
P.O. Box 1146
Sacramento

Riverside Marina
Engine
5804 Riverside Blvd.
Sacramento

Stan's Freeport Baitshop & Marina
Engine, Hull
8250 Freeport Blvd.
Freeport

Tower Bridge Marina
Engine, Hull, Prop & Shaft
P.O. Box 703
W. Sacramento

Village Marina
Engine, Hull, Prop & Shaft
Rt. 3, Box 385
Sacramento

Facilities not located on the water *

*A small Sacramento river landing
where modern boats are moored
alongside an old passenger carrier*

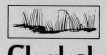 # Sacramento-
Clarksburg Area

Your Log Notes:

On the way up to the capital.

A Delta Afterview and Acknowledgements

It is the fashion these days for the author of a book to make his thank yous as brief as possible. When I was almost finished with this book, I told my publishers that my acknowledgments could not be confined to just a few words on a part of a page. I explained that in keeping with the whole philosophy of the region about which I was writing, its warmth and friendliness, its spirit of helpfulness, I would have a number of people to thank and a number of things to say about them. Now, at the end of this book, I want to do just that.

Men, Ships and the Sea is the National Geographic Society's exceptional history of the entire span of boating since the day that man learned that logs, bark and hides will float. The authors closed the text portion of this remarkable work with this quotation from Kenneth Grahame's delightful *The Wind in the Willows:* "There is **nothing,** absolutely nothing, half so much worth doing as simply messing about in boats. Simply messing."

For centuries, this has been the philosophic consensus of many literary men of the seas and the unsalted waters alike.

Whether one travels by boat to far horizons, or takes up an afternoon on the anchor line in a quiet nearby harbor, whether one travels to the water's edge by auto or goes so far to embrace historic ports that he lives aboard for weeks, the result is the same—only by degrees. When the water brings unlimited pleasure to a family crew, distance, the kind of shoreline, the degree of solitude, do not necessarily matter.

The "messing about in boats" philosophy fits the California Delta and the boating people who love it—residents or visitors—to a T. And I hope the reader will forgive me if I insist that, in this particular case, applying the lexicon of the Delta, the T must stand for tule.

So to all those in the Delta who joined me in messing about in boats in their beautiful country, I say thank you. I can only hope they enjoyed it as much as I did.

In the last years of his adventurous life, the late Erle Stanley Gardner discovered the joys of the Delta's rivers, sloughs and bayous. He settled into several boat ownerships in that area and kept his craft in their native ports. In due course of time, he wrote three books about the California Delta. The facile creator of the famous Perry Mason series of courtroom and detective novels and television scripts wrote these three books in a very personal vein befitting the warmth of his feeling for the easy, friendly life. Gardner loved the water, loved adventure, loved sailing to strange lands and entering exotic ports. Yet to him the Delta was an exceptional place of long afternoons of catfishing and relaxing. He marveled that, just minutes away from the dock, he was living a new, leisurely, carefree life. He couldn't find words enough for telling of his Delta friends, the hundreds of inland waterways that sparkle in the sunlight, the good cheer, courtesy and open-handed hospitality of the people of the area.

In 1948, as an editor on the magazine *Pacific Motor Boat* (*SEA & Pacific Motor Boat*'s predecessor), I had corresponded with Gardner to obtain his permission to reprint an article called *Log of the Landlubber* which he had written for PMB in 1924. In actual fact, we did reprint the article in its original form and Gardner was quite delighted to have it appear again. By this time he was a famous author and the Perry Mason series had been born.

Thus when Erle Stanley Gardner began writing about the California Delta and his adventures there, I naturally acquired his books and enjoyed his Delta as I was enjoying my own. I have shared Gardner's enthusiasm for—and enjoyment of—this delightful Northern California cruising area. Any who love the Delta, who cruise and tarry there, owe something to Gardner and my own acknowledgment of this indebtedness has dictated Gardner's place in this book.

In addition, this book owes much, and I am personally indebted, to many persons, groups and organizations who have been generous with time, information, materials and all manner of help. I cannot name them all but I must call the roll of as many as I can.

Thanks to these skippers and yachtsmen, gentlemen all:

Tim Moseley, Staff Commodore of the St. Francis YC, San Francisco.
Thomas A. Short, Staff Commodore of the St. Francis YC and PCYA, San Francisco.
Richard W. Smith, skipper of the *Pacific Gypsy*, San Francisco, Mokelumne River and Sacramento.
John Soares, skipper of the cruiser *Fiddlesticks*, of Antioch and Spindrift Marina.
Paul Wright, of Glendale, yachtsman and Power Squadrons' cruise leader.
Al Eames, of Antioch and Georgiana Slough.
Tom Barnes, yachtsman, of Discovery Bay and Stockton.

George Sherrill, yachtsman, Newport Bay.

Douglas Boswell, yachtsman, Past Commodore of PCYA and perennial father to the Northern California Inter-Club Association, of San Rafael.

Jack Bailey, skipper of the *Bunty Lawless*, of Spindrift Marina.

Leonard N. Atwood, skipper of the *Yankee K.*, of San Francisco. (Publisher's note: Deceased, January, 1972.)

My special gratitude to all of the officers and members of the Delta yacht clubs and the specialty clubs of the area. In particular, I must mention these staff officers:

Eugene N. Perry, Cupertino	Sam Martin, Oakland
Frances Osgood, Mokelumne YC	William H. Gray, Jr., Napa
Jack L. Hall, Santa Rosa	Robert Holmes, Walnut Creek
Al Simaz, Orinda	Richard H. Salsman, Saratoga
Edwin Miller, Orinda	Anders MacDonald, Concord

Many Delta area civic leaders and businessmen, among them many yachtsmen and men who have devoted a good share of their lives to boating activities, gave selflessly of time, effort and much valuable information which would not have been obtainable elsewhere. I must mention:

Jack Baumann, owner of Delta Marina Yacht Harbor, Rio Vista.

Myron M. Brown, Chairman of the Board, The Bank of Alex Brown, Walnut Grove.

William Boyd, real estate broker, Bethel Island.

Gene Calcagno, Calcagno Yacht Sales, Stockton.

Jess Crowe, Spindrift Marina and member of Spindrift YC.

Lloyd Korth, Korth's Pirates Lair Marina, Korth's Harbor.

George Marr and Constance (Marr) King, and the Marr family, of Locke.

John Moore, Moore's Riverboat Restaurant and Yacht Haven.

Manuel ("Mo") Morias, Giusti's, Walnut Grove.

Harry Schilling and Harry Schilling, Jr., Spindrift Marina.

John W. Thieme, President of Delta Cruz Houseboat Rentals and former President of the Northern California Houseboat Rental Association, Bethel Island.

Ed Wilson, B&W Marina Resort, Isleton.

Chuck Philippart, Delta Sportsman marine store, Bethel Island.

Angelo and Mrs. Palumbo, Korth's Harbor.

In many ways this has been a Delta picture book with a bit of history thrown in for good measure. In the course of working on the book, I had many fine assists from organizations and individuals in the area of historical information, access to wonderful photo collections, both public and private, and chart and map navigational information. In this category, I must especially thank:

Rolph G. (Dutch) Bremer, Isleton, for permitting use of the Bremer collection of photographs and other historical data.

The inimitable sources of The Bancroft Library, University of California at Berkeley.

Charles K. Davis, Isleton, for use of the Davis collection of photos and historical information on the Delta levees.

Sharon Steiner, the Plowlands, photography, Walnut Grove.

Captain Ed Morgan, *Delta King* restoration project, Sacramento.

The Delta Region Facility Chart, published by Delta Marina Yacht Harbor, Inc., Rio Vista—a great overall quick-reference chart available on marine supply counters throughout the Delta.

The Weekend Outdoor Map for Delta rivers and sloughs, Box 878, Oakland, 94604—best quick guide I have found to fishing spots and fishing specialty resorts and landings in the Delta country.

The California State Automobile Association; Robert W. Graver, Assistant Vice President, Public Services Dept., San Francisco, for permission to use their fine maps of the San Joaquin and Sacramento valley areas.

The United States Department of Commerce for Nautical Charts 5527-SC and 5528-SC covering the Sacramento and San Joaquin rivers; hydrography and topography by the Coast and Geodetic Survey, available at official marine chart outlets.

Mercury Marine of Fond du Lac, Wisconsin; Evinrude Motors of Milwaukee, Wisconsin; Chrysler Corporation's Marine Division, Detroit, Michigan; and Johnson Motors of Waukeegan, Illinois; for their courtesies in providing equipment assistance for flexible coverage of the Delta waterways.

Was there ever a man who wrote a book who didn't owe a great, great deal to his fellow writers? This author freely and fully confesses how much he owes to the several other authors, historians and, not incidentally, lovers of things marine who went this way before him. Let me mention:

Richard A. (Bob) Miller, author of *Fortune Built by Gun*, Mansion Publishing Company, Sacramento, for consents to use illustrations and data from his collection.

Roger Minick, and his photographer/historian, David Bohn, author of *Delta West*, Scrimshaw Press, Berkeley; a deluxe limited edition book.

Rivers of California, a booklet published by Pacific Gas and Electric Co., San Francisco—a concise, able history and description of the state's rivers at their sources.

George H. Harlan and Clement Fisher, Jr., authors of *Walking Beams and Paddle Wheels*, published by Bay Books, San Francisco. Special thanks for giving me the chance to understand the propulsion machinery of the Bay ferries.

Helen McBurney, author, newspaperwoman and publisher of *Bay & Delta Yachtsman*, Rio Vista, a pleasure-boating periodical . . . my gratitude for her generous assistance with my project and her many introductions to knowledgeable people in the Delta.

Jerry MacMullen, marine historian/author, San Diego, for his fine dissertation on specifications for steamboats on California rivers in his book *Paddle-Wheel Days in California*, Stanford University Press at Stanford. I recommend this to yachting Deltaphiles who will thrill, as I did, to MacMullen's accounts of steamboating on the Sacramento and the San Joaquin.

The publisher and staff of *SEA* Magazine for making available to me information in the 1972 Handbook.

Much reference material a writer uses isn't written down but is given to him orally. In this context, my deep gratitude to Ping K. Lee, owner of Big Store, Walnut Grove, for the history of the Chinese settlers—derived from his own studies and observations and the stories handed down to him by his pioneering father and mother.

I have already acknowledged my indebtedness to the late Erle Stanley Gardner. Let me list here his Delta books with the recommendation they belong in every Delta yachtsman's library: *The World of Water* (1964), *Gypsy Days on the Delta* (1967) and *Drifting Down the Delta* (1969); Publisher: William Morrow and Company, New York.

And finally my publishers and their representative, Ray Poulter, and his fine crew of very good, talented people who worked with me . . . thanks to Kent Sanctuary for book design and layout direction, Donna Blistein for special graphics, cover and dustjacket design; Tom Dorsaneo for all his production expertise; Peggy Boyer and Barbara Hampson for fine editing; they've been a great crew on a long Delta cruise.

So there it is. Good cruising!

Bob Walters

Long Beach, California
March, 1972